Glass Painting

Naazish Chouglay

The Art of Crafts

First published in 1999 by
The Crowood Press Ltd
Ramsbury, Marlborough
Wiltshire SN8 2HR

British Library Cataloguing in Publication Data

A catalogue record for this book is available from the British Library.

ISBN 1 86126 227 2

Acknowledgements
I would like to take this opportunity to thank all my friends and relatives, whose
support and encouragement have made this book possible.

I could not have progressed in my hobby without help from my partner
Ayesha and friend Noorjehan, who have supported me in all my glass painting
ventures, Tasnim who introduced me to glass painting, and Bahar who always
provides me with artistic inspiration.

I would like to thank Gerry, who made the windows for the book, and Jonathan,
who did the photography so beautifully.

A special thanks to my parents, Gulnar and Hasan, who came over from India
especially to support me while I wrote this book.

Last but not least, this book could not have been written without the constant
support of my patient husband Akbar, and loving encouragement from my children Karishma and Rayhan, who both innocently say 'Mummy, you are the best
painter'.

Photographic Acknowledgements
Thanks to Farook Faquih Architects and Jonathan Sands for the photography.

The photograph on page 9 has been reproduced by the permission of Victoria
and Albert Museum, UK.

The illustration on page 54 has been reproduced by the permission of Salaman-
der Press, UK.

Typeset by D & N Publishing
Membury Business Park, Lambourn Woodlands
Hungerford, Berkshire.

Printed and bound by Leo Paper Products, China.

Contents

Introduction

It is difficult to imagine a home without the benefits of glass, and without the brightness and protection it brings. Natural glass is as old as the universe and the use of glass in building goes back to Roman times. However, the art of stained glass is fairly young, having developed over the last thousand years. Stained glass has been closely associated with history, religion, social change and scientific discovery.

In the suburban house-building boom at the turn of the century, it was the front door and the front parlour windows that contained stained glass, both as a form of window dressing and sometimes, together with drawn net curtains, as a form of privacy. Art Deco influenced the simple designs of such windows, and it is interesting how the fashion for decorative glazing that started in the major towns spread over a number of years to other parts of the country.

Traditional glass painting is an exacting technique that requires considerable expertise and knowledge of the subject, as well as requiring specialized equipment such as a kiln. It is different from many other forms of painting and the end result depends on various factors such as the type of glass used, the temperature of the kiln and the method of application of the paints.

Traditional stained glass and glass painting can be imitated, by using transparent glass paints and imitation lead. With new developments in outliners, and with the improvement in the quality of glass paints, painting on glass has taken on a whole new dimension. It is no longer a craft that imitates stained glass, but a whole new art in itself.

GLASS PAINTING

Glass painting is a simple and enjoyable craft to learn, and so long as you follow the basic techniques the range of things you can decorate is unlimited. The appeal of glass painting lies in its simplicity and originality. It is quick to do, inexpensive and gives hours of pleasure.

There are few crafts that offer such scope for creativity, yet require so few specialist tools and do not need a workshop. All you need are a table, good light, a few tools and some carefully selected supports on which to paint.

Glass painting is a very relaxing and therapeutic hobby, which everybody can enjoy, whatever their age.

One of the common fears that most people have before they start a craft is that they are not very creative. However, once they have got started, most people find they are filled with creative ideas that can be wonderfully and personally expressed. All they need is encouragement and confidence.

Over the years that I have been teaching glass painting, I have noticed that many people are reluctant to begin painting because they are worried that they cannot paint or draw. The beauty of glass painting is that because you start off by painting on transparent materials such as acetate sheets and glass, you can trace designs before painting. Your initial fear is overcome and then of course there is no looking back. You are hooked!

1 The Story of Glass

Glass has been made and employed by man for nearly three-thousand five-hundred years to create a wide and varied range of objects for both domestic and industrial purposes. It is a highly versatile and flexible material, which is easily manipulated and shaped when it is hot. Clear and colourless like rock crystal, opaque or richly coloured to simulate semi-precious stones, glass is able to sustain numerous forms of decoration, including cutting, engraving, gilding, enamelling, painting and various other forms of decoration. It has always provided a medium for artistic expression.

Three things are needed for making glass: silica, alkali and heat. Silica, such as sand, quartz or flint, is fused with an alkali such as soda or potash. The latter acts as a flux, assisting the silica to melt and encouraging the mixture to combine more readily.

Glass is found in nature as obsidian, a blackish-grey, somewhat translucent substance that is formed from lava, and which exhibits much the same properties found in man-made glass. However, while both obsidian and alabaster, have in the past been used to make windows, neither have the same extraordinary quality of near-transparency possessed by man-made glass, and as a consequence they do not have the same transcendental overtones.

HISTORY OF GLASS

The exact history of the discovery of how to manufacture glass is not known, but Pliny, the historian writing in the first century AD, tells this story of how glass was first invented:

Apparently a group of Syrian merchants were transporting a load of natron, which is made of sodium salts and found in dried lake beds. They camped for the night on the sandy shores of a lake. They lit a fire and placed their cooking-pots next to it, supporting them on the cakes of natron. In the morning they were surprised to find that with the heat of the fire, the natron and sand had fused to form glass. This may be legend, but there is no doubt that the Syrians were accomplished glass-makers.

Glass has had a strangely intermittent history. Glass beads are known from about the middle of the third millennium BC. Hollow vessels in glass dating from around 1500BC have been found, but the craft died out almost completely after three centuries. It was then revived in Mesopotamia and Syria in the ninth century and slowly spread westwards and northwards. Glass-making arrived in Alexandria soon after the foundation of the city in 332BC. This became the most important centre of production, as it was for many luxury crafts during the Hellenistic era.

Among the ancient Egyptian vessels which have survived are some in a rich range of opaque colours. Egyptian glass-makers knew how to create various shades of blue – a pervasive and highly favoured colour – as well as green, yellow, violet, white, black and bright red. There were two reasons for their marked preference for coloured wares. First to disguise the natural green, brown and purple tints brought about by impurities, and secondly to imitate semi-precious stones.

The art of glass flourished under the Romans and the discovery of glass-blowing by human lungs was the greatest step in the history of glass-making. It transformed glass making, and large quantities of wares could now be produced easily and cheaply. This method of producing glass was employed right until the nineteenth century.

The Romans also discovered a relatively colourless glass which was created by the addition of manganese oxide, at least 1,500 years after the discovery of glass-colouring techniques. It is also interesting to note that nearly all the basic methods of decorating blown glass by blowing or cutting had been developed before the fourth century in Egypt and Syria.

Although not a natural substance, glass was regarded as magical and even divine during the Middle Ages. Indeed, to take a base material such as sand, and by an irreversible process, purify it into a new and nobler form was like alchemy, but demonstrably more successful. Glass-makers, firing their wood-burning furnaces, could turn the lowest of the elements, earth, into a durable and practical substance, glass. It was the ability of glass to transmit light, to be looked through and looked at, which made it so special.

Today, glass is so familiar a material that we treat it with scant respect, but in the Middle Ages it was precious and coloured glass even more so. In general, it was only to be found in churches, being much too difficult and costly to obtain for domestic use. The earliest window glass was made either by casting into a shallow mould, or by blowing an elongated bubble, splitting down the length of the cylinder thus made, and opening it out to form a flat sheet. This is known as 'antique' glass and is one of the types of glass most suitable for stained glass.

From the twelfth century onwards, the making of glass vessels took second place to the production of window glass. The fifteenth century saw the development of enamelled coloured vessels, and clear crystal glass was discovered in the seventeenth century. Bohemian coloured cut glass and flashed glass became very prominent in the nineteenth century.

The first great technical development of glass since the invention of glass-blowing took place in 1825 in the United States of America with the discovery of how to make pressed glass. This facilitated the mass-production of standard items. Another major contribution to the mass-production of glass was the development of mechanically blown glass. But undoubtedly the most important technical development of glass has been the

creation of various types of heat-resistant glass, the best being known as Pyrex.

Today, every stage of glass manufacture has become mechanized and continuous. The manufacture of household glass has been revolutionized by computer control, and a modern machine can produce over 100,000 glass vessels a day. The overall result is that there is now a greater variety of household glass than there ever has been.

HISTORY OF GLASS DECORATION

Apart from the colouring of glass, which is a form of decoration in itself, numerous other methods of ornamentation have been developed and are continuing to develop. For example, plain clear or coloured glass surfaces can be embellished by enamelling, gilding or cold painting to create a variety of monochrome or polychrome effects.

Enamelling

Enamelling is an ancient glass-decorating technique, which was practised as early as the fifteenth century BC. It differs from cold painting in that the colours are permanent and fused to the glass by refiring it in a muffle kiln.

Cold Painting

Cold painting has also been a very popular method of decorating glass. The technique involves the painting of coloured pigments onto the glass surface, with no subsequent firing. The colours employed are oil- or lacquer-based and do not require any additional heating to develop their tone or fuse them to the surface. The disadvantage of using this method is that the decoration can be worn away or damaged easily, and many old pieces that have been cold painted have lost their original designs. Cold painting was frequently reserved for those wares which were too big to be placed in the kiln, or too fragile to sustain a second firing. In addition, the technique was employed by amateur decorators who had no access to a kiln.

Gilding

Gilding is achieved by the application of gold as paint, powder or foil to the surface or the underside of the glass, which is then fired in a kiln. This refiring creates a variety of effects on the glass. Gilding by painting onto the surface of the object was frequently combined with enamelling (both subsequently fired at low temperatures and fused to the exterior), as on Islamic mosque lamps and late fifteenth-century Venetian commemorative wares. In the late eighteenth and nineteenth centuries, gilding appeared as the only form of decoration employed by English decorators.

Gold leaf has been employed since Roman times, when it was engraved with religious motifs and placed under a second protective layer of colourless glass. This was called 'fondi d'oro', and was revived in the eighteenth century in Germany, where gold between glass decoration appeared on glass tumblers and goblets. Gold in powdered form, or as a thin foil, could also be fused to the outside surface of the glass, if mixed with an adhesive such as honey and fired at low temperatures to achieve reasonable permanence.

Cold gilding is a method similar to cold painting, where gold is applied on the surface with no subsequent firing. It is a very impermanent method. The gold leaf is laid over some sort of oil or gum on the glass and simply dried. It is very fragile and can be easily rubbed or washed off.

Etching and Frosting

Etching and frosting are relatively new forms of glass decoration and were not employed extensively before the nineteenth century. The technique involves the use of hydrofluoric acid, which eats into the walls of the glass, leaving behind a clear, frosted or pitted surface, depending upon the strength of the acid and the length of the treatment. First, the object is covered with an acid-resistant substance such as wax or varnish. A design is then drawn into this coating with a pointed instrument. The hydrofluoric acid, usually mixed with potassium fluoride and water, is applied to the object. The acid attacks the exposed areas of glass, where the wash has been removed. The glass is finally washed to reveal the etched surface design. French Art Nouveau designers, including Emile Gallé, employed this method of decoration during the nineteenth century. Hydrofluoric acid is a very dangerous material and stringent safety precautions have to be observed when using it.

Sand Blasting

Sand blasting was invented in 1870 by Tilgman, but has been employed only recently for the decoration of glass. The object is first covered with a protective mask which exposes parts of the underlying glass according to the required design. The whole glass is then subjected to blasts of sand (or other abrasives such as powdered iron or flint) projected at high velocity from a special gun. The result is a finely frosted effect, which varies according to the type of abrasive used and the force at which it is expelled. The French designer René Lalique employed sand-blasting for decorative purposes and for the 'R Lalique' trademark.

HISTORY OF STAINED GLASS AND GLASS PAINTING

Most homes have at least one window that would benefit from the magic of stained glass. The opportunities are particularly rich in doors, stairwells, bathrooms, kitchens, internal screens and conservatories. Some works are designed to obscure the outside view, wholly or partially, while some create a kind of dialogue between interior and exterior – for instance, the use of plant motifs would be an obvious allusion to a garden glimpsed through the design. Stained glass used ornamentally as a door surround can create a degree of privacy, yet at the same time have a warm, welcoming ambience.

The art of stained glass probably originated in the Middle East and perhaps first took the form of the infilling of small holes pierced in walls. It is also probable that the origins of the art are linked with enamelling. By the twelfth century the technique of stained glass was fairly widely known.

Stained glass windows were erected in large numbers from the twelfth century onwards in the large and imposing late Romanesque and early Gothic cathedrals and abbeys of north-western Europe. The coloured glass was supplied by factories throughout the region. It is likely that much of the glass was exported freely from country to country.

Originally, the patterns for stained glass windows were abstract, but by the mid-eleventh century panels of glass were arranged to represent figures. By the twelfth and thirteenth centuries the art of making stained glass windows for cathedrals and windows reached its peak of excellence. The windows were made up of a mosaic of variously coloured crown glass onto which details of faces, folds of drapery or leaves of plants were painted in opaque enamel. These windows were composed of an enormous number of small pieces of glass leaded together, which made the windows very heavy.

During the fourteenth century, technical advances were made and larger panels of coloured glass were used in the windows. A transparent yellow surface stain was developed from the sulphide of silver. This yellow staining was painted and subsequently fired onto the surface of the glass, ranging in tone from a pale lemon to deep orange (according to the potency of the solution and kiln conditions). Both these developments meant that the windows became lighter, and the role of the glass painter, who picked out detail in enamels, increased significantly. The number of pieces of glass leaded together also decreased considerably.

At the end of the fourteenth century the art of glass painting received an onward impulse when Jean of Bruges invented the technique of cold painting. To him is also attributed the discovery of enamel colours for glass painting, other than the brown enamel already in use.

In the fifteenth century it became possible to pick out fine details in white on coloured glass, due to the development of abrasion of sheets of flashed glass. The influence of the developments taking place in painting and drawing began to be felt, as was shown in the improved drawing, the greater employment of light and shade and the execution of faces with greater delicacy and care.

Finally, by the sixteenth century, transparent enamel pigments had been discovered. These could be painted onto regular-shaped sheets of clear white glass, thus reducing the number of coloured glass pieces required for the windows. During this period, the art of glass painting reached its apex. The drawings were

accurate and the colours beautiful and well blended. However, by the end of the sixteenth century glass painting had rapidly deteriorated. The use of enamel paints became excessive and glass painting became a manufacture instead of an art. During the seventeenth and eighteenth centuries the art declined, except in the Netherlands.

There was a revival of the art in the second half of the nineteenth century, not only as a result of the refurbishment of old churches and the erection of new ones, but also in keeping with contemporary tastes for a return to craftsmanship and the revival of mediaevalist ideals. In England Sir Edward Burne-Jones and William Morris designed many windows, and revived the art, by establishing a glass-staining studio in London in 1861. In the USA, John La Farge and later Tiffany became famous for their art glass windows, many of which were made for the homes of the wealthy, as well as for churches. In France, stained glass became very popular during the Art Nouveau period, based on designs produced by artists like Henri Matisse and Ferdinand Leger.

The heyday of secular stained glass was the end of the nineteenth century when it was wholeheartedly embraced by most of the famous architects and designers, including Charles Rennie Mackintosh, Adolf Loos, Otto Wagner, Hector Guimard, Antoni Gaudi and Louis Comfort Tiffany. Most of these figures were part of a mainly ornamental tradition whose impact lasted well into the twentieth century.

The most influential stained glass movement in recent times started in Germany in the post-war years. Its origins go further back, but it was the church-building boom in West Germany, in the aftermath of the war that impelled the medium to catch up with the advances already seen in other visual arts. Perhaps

it was also an underlying need to make a clean break with the past that motivated patrons to seek work that was truly contemporary.

The current trend for building large complexes under glass, such as shopping malls, provides opportunities for works on a large scale. Stained glass can also transform spaces that are in continuous occupation, such as offices; here the intention is often to humanize a mass-produced environment.

TRADITIONAL STAINED GLASS

The craft of the glazier, like most crafts, seems to have run in families, thus facilitating the keeping of trade secrets. Most stained glass, however, was produced by commercially run firms, and these, if there were enough of them, were organized into guilds. London had a guild of glass painters by 1328.

The site where the stained glass is to be placed is measured and assessed, the design created and then a small sketch drawn to scale. This is enlarged into a full-sized cartoon, which is then traced onto a transparent paper to make cut lines. The glass is cut piece by piece, the selection of the colours being a vitally important part of the design. They are placed on the cartoon so that the main drawing lines may be traced onto them using special brushes, and the drawing is often fired at this stage. Tones and textures are added using iron oxide with powdered glass. They are used for defining the details of faces, hands, drapery and so forth and for 'matting' so as to modify the colour. Highlights or patterns are removed with stiff brushes, known as 'scrubs' or by using a needle or any such pointed instrument for very thin work. Sponges, fingers or splashes of oil or water are used to give texture. The pieces are then fired again at a temperature of about 620° centigrade. The process of firing fixes the paint permanently.

If any of the glass is to be stained yellow, this is done last. Unlike paint, which remains on the surface, stain will actually penetrate the glass once it is fired at about 520°C. The glass is then leaded, soldered and cemented. The leads are blacked and brushed as a dark lead line enhances the design and enriches the colour.

If the window is more than 3ft (1m) high, it has to be supported horizontally with saddle bars, which are made of iron or non-rusting metal. As the size of the window increases, it becomes necessary to apply vertical support as well. Thus the practical necessity of supporting windows had a considerable influence on their design.

OTHER STAINED GLASS TECHNIQUES

We tend to think of leading as an essential part of stained glass, but some modern windows are made with no lead at all. They are constructed by embedding slab glass in concrete or epoxy resins. Slab glass is far thicker than the glass normally used for leaded windows. Whole curtain walls of embedded stained glass are possible as long as they do not have to be load-bearing; it becomes difficult to say what is structure and what is decoration. The window becomes very much part of the architecture.

The Durability of Stained Glass

Though stained glass is both durable and resilient, and stands up remarkably well to the conditions to which it is generally exposed, it is still vulnerable.

The degree to which glass erodes varies surprisingly. It is not always the most ancient glass that presents the greatest problems. Of two pieces of glass of similar date in the same panel, one may be completely clear and healthy, and the other hopelessly decayed. It depends on their chemical constituents when first made. Nineteenth-century glass may also be found to have decayed. Opinions vary about what is the main cause of the corrosion of glass – from water, to the spread of lichen, to sulphur dioxide in the atmosphere.

Lead is less durable than glass and after a century or so decays, and the solder at the joints cracks. In addition, there are the problems of breakages, whether accidental or as a result of vandalism.

2 Materials and Equipment

Glass painting is one of the fastest growing crafts in recent years and there is a wide range of paints available in the market. Glass paints are epoxy paints which are transparent, and which when painted on supports like transparent glass or acetate allow light to pass through them.

Glass paints are easily available from craft shops and DIY shops. The paints are generally air-drying, although there are some which require baking. These paints can be applied to most surfaces such as glass, plastic, metal, shells, stone and wood. However, absorbent surfaces like wood would have to be coated with a lacquer before painting over them. The best way to introduce yourself to this hobby is by painting on acetate sheets, glasses and jam jars. Once you have done two or three basic projects, you can then invest in vases, bottles and other glassware. As your skills develop, you can then be adventurous and perhaps paint a window or door panel.

The paints are semi-permanent and as with most colouring media, a gradual loss of colour may occur over a period of time, and the colours will fade when exposed to strong sunlight, and peel away if left to soak for long in water.

However, on the other hand, they are easy to use, easy to clean and great fun to experiment with.

With proper care and protection painted works of art will give years of pleasure. When painting a surface exposed to the elements, the best way to protect the paint is to seal it between two layers of glass. This will preserve the painting from deterioration caused by exposure.

WORK AREA

Your work area or studio should be light and well aired. The work table should be at a comfortable height. Keep it clear of anything other than the items you are going to need when glass painting, and make sure you have all the things you require to hand before beginning any project.

You should protect your clothes with an apron or an old shirt, and cover your work surface with an old cloth or papers and follow common-sense procedures to minimize damage from any accidents. The surface of the supports must be clean, dry and free from dust particles and residues before any paint is applied.

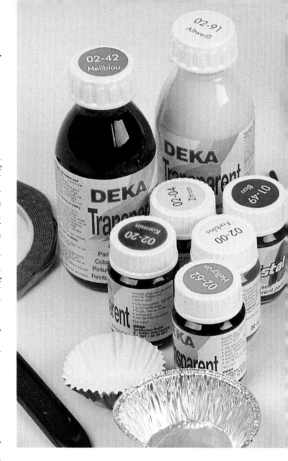

MATERIALS

Craft shops are seductive places, and once back home you could find yourself lumbered with a lot of equipment and materials you do not really need. Three bottles of the primary colours, a black outliner tube, a brush and some acetate sheet should be sufficient to get you started. Then as you begin to enjoy glass painting you can add to your range of colours and outliner tubes. Caps of bottles or foil cups can be used as palettes, and materials such as old rags, paper towels and cotton buds can be collected from around the house.

PAINTS

Paint has been defined as any liquid or semi-liquid substance applied to any surface to protect it from corrosion or decay, or to give it colour or gloss, or both. It is a mixture of opaque or semi-opaque substances (pigments) with liquids which may be applied to a surface by means of a brush or a painting machine, or by dipping. It has the property of forming an adherent coating on the surface it is applied to.

The variety of glass paints is growing to meet the demands of this increasingly popular hobby. These paints are either solvent-based or water-based acrylic lacquers containing dyestuffs and/or organic pigments. They have been especially formulated for the decoration of glass and other transparent materials such as plastic.

Some of the more popular brands are Pebeo, Le Franc and Bourgeois, Deka, Marabu and Decorfin. These paints are either solvent-based or water-based. Having worked with all the different types of paints, I prefer Deka transparent paints, which are solvent-based. The solvent-based paints flow smoothly, have a velvety finish, are consistent and mix very well. Having said that, each artist develops his or her own preference for a particular brand of paint depending on cost, availability and quality of paints. When choosing your paints and brushes, even though expensive doesn't necessarily mean the best, cheap, poor quality materials will only frustrate you and your interest in glass painting will likely soon wane.

Water-Based Paints and Solvent-Based Paints

The function of medium in paints is:

- to bind, surround and coat each pigment particle to give a workable mixture that will adhere to the painting surface;
- to act as a glue;
- to add 'character' to the paint – i.e. to give it a gloss or matt finish, or to

make it opaque or transparent. At the same time, the additional medium may improve the handling qualities of the paint.

Solvent-based paints are brighter and smoother. These paints are lightfast and do not fade easily. However, the smell of the solvent can be quite overpowering and therefore not suitable for people who are uncomfortable with strong smells. These paints must always be used in a well-ventilated room. The solvents used differ from manufacturer to manufacturer, and in most cases you cannot mix paints of two different brands. It is therefore advisable to choose one brand, and stick to it. Solvent-based paints also dry and harden quicker than water-based paints.

Due to regulations with regard to the use of solvents, water-based paints must be used when you are working with children. The quality of water-based paints has improved dramatically over the years and when used on acetate, the effects of these paints are as good as the solvent-based paints. Water based glass paints and solvent-based paints do not mix.

The drying time of the paints varies from manufacturer to manufacturer, as well as according to the thickness of the paint used. On average, the paints take approximately half an hour to an hour to dry, and overnight to harden. Almost all glass paints are air-drying unless otherwise stated. If baking is recommended by the manufacturer, follow the instructions given. As most paints are air-drying, never leave the paint bottles exposed to air.

A few years ago, only specialist craft shops and DIY shops sold glass paints, but due to the growing popularity of this craft, they are now easily available in most art and craft shops, through mail order and even in stationery shops. There are many types of starter kits available as well.

Thinners

The purpose of a thinner is to make paint spread further and to make it easier to apply.

White spirit is the common thinner, and it can be used with most solvent-based glass paints. However, depending on the brand of paint you are using, it is better to use the manufacturer's recommended thinner when using solvent-based paints, as they work better when thinning and cleaning brushes.

Preferably use distilled water as a thinner for water-based paints, as well as for cleaning brushes, although ordinary tap water can be used.

Outliner Tubes

The outliner tube is also called cerne relief or liquid lead. The name 'liquid

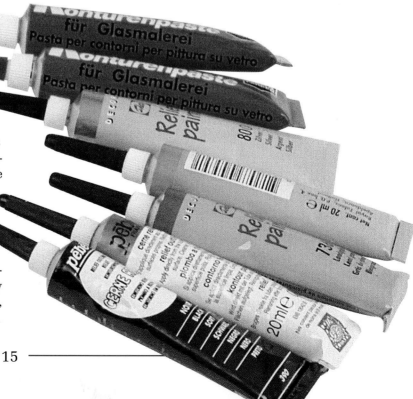

lead' for this material is quite deceptive because it does not contain any lead. The outliner is an acrylic paste which is available in tubes. The tubes have a nozzle which helps to control the thickness of the outliner as you apply it. Outliner tubes come in black, imitation lead, gold and silver colour. Recent additions have been bronze and copper colours along with different shades of gold and silver. Ceramic paint outliners are available in a wider range of colours than glass paint outliners, and these combine very effectively with glass paints. Like most of the paints, the outliner is also air-drying and takes approximately an hour or so to dry, hardening overnight. The drying time of the outliners also differs from manufacturer to manufacturer. Thickness of the paste affects the drying time as well – the thinner the outline, the quicker it will dry.

BRUSHES

Brushes are the main tool of the painter and they are used above all for applying paint, although sometimes they are also used as drawing instruments. Brushes come in a wide variety of shapes and sizes and are made from different types of hair or bristle. Certain brush types are suited to particular types of paint, and particular methods of application.

Hair Types

There are many different hair types used in brushes, but the very best of the hairs is sable obtained from the sable marten, a mink-like creature. Sable brushes are delightful to work with, and can be made with an extremely fine point, which because of its strength and flexibility allows precise control over the paint as it is set down.

These specially fashioned points can make the most delicate lines and strokes. In addition, they are constructed to hold the paint well, and so spread it with ease and fluency. The advantage of a sable brush over most of the other types is that it responds to the touch with great sensitivity, effectively becoming an extension of the hand. However, these brushes are also expensive and so must be used carefully.

Squirrel is softer than sable but cheaper and vastly inferior. A large brush made of squirrel will perform better than a small one. Amongst the many other hair types are pony, ox, camel, bristle, fitch, goat and badger.

Synthetic Hair

Synthetic hair was introduced in order to overcome the high cost and increasing rarity of good natural hair. These brushes imitate the qualities of sable and bristle and have a tapering filament.

Synthetic brushes are relatively inexpensive and are particularly desirable for painting in acrylics because they are able to withstand repeated cleaning in strong solvents and are hard wearing. Their low cost means that they can simply be thrown away if cleaning proves difficult. However, it is not advisable to buy very cheap brushes, because they have no spring in them and more often than not the bristles fall out.

Brushes come in many shapes, but watercolour brushes which taper at the top to a good point are the most suitable type for glass painting.

Brushes are a very personal tool. Every painter seems to develop his or her individual preference and what suits one artist often only proves to be totally unsuitable for another.

A good quality fine brush, not necessarily made of hair, should be sufficient for your needs as a beginner, but as you progress you will need different types of brushes for different types of work. A No. 2 synthetic brush is sufficient to get you started in this hobby. As you progress, you can add a No. 7 watercolour brush for broad work. Other sizes can be added later.

Foam brushes are ideal for painting large surfaces like glass bottles and so on, where the whole surface has to be painted; 1in (25mm) foam brushes used by silk painters are ideal for this purpose.

Looking after brushes is part of painting and if treated properly they will give good service and do their job well. The best way to clean brushes used with solvent-based paints is to suspend them in the manufacturer's recommended cleaner or in white spirit. Water-based paints can be cleaned easily in warm soapy water.

Washing brushes after use is a more thorough operation than cleaning them during work. It does not mean a swirl round in clean water. Colour has a habit of remaining deeply embedded in the hair of the brush and must be removed, or it will ruin the brush in time. Therefore make it a practice to wash them with warm water and mild soap (not a detergent). Lather in the palm of the hand, watch all the hidden paint emerge, rinse well in plenty of warm water before allowing them to dry upright in a jar or bottle. In the case of solvent-based, this is the final clean after the brushes have been washed in brush cleaner.

If brushes are unfortunately encrusted with dried paint, you can try soaking them in warm water for a few hours. Warm water will soften the paint and then it may be removed by easing it off carefully with the fingers. Avoid using any kind of sharp implement because you may damage the hairs irrevocably, and once the point or edge of a brush is damaged, the brush is virtually useless.

IMITATION LEAD

Lead cames are used in the framework of stained glass windows. A lead came is either H or U shaped in cross-section and the glass is fitted into the channel of the came, which is then soldered together at the junctions.

Imitation lead, or self-adhesive lead was developed to imitate the lead cames used in stained glass windows. Imitation lead is available in DIY shops and craft shops. These are strips of lead with adhesive backing which can be stuck directly onto glass, before painting the glass. The lead is flexible and can be stretched or cut to size, and if necessary even cut into thinner strips. As lead is poisonous always wear gloves when handling it.

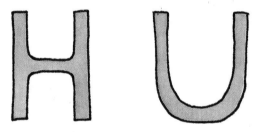

COPPER FOIL

Copper foil is a thin tape with an adhesive back that is wrapped around the glass pieces. The foiled pieces of glass are then soldered together into shapes or patterns. This method is attributed to the inventiveness of Louis Comfort Tiffany, whose name is associated with the delicate 'Tiffany' lampshades and windows of the nineteenth century.

Copper foil is conveniently available in sealed bags ranging from $\frac{3}{32}$in to $\frac{1}{2}$in widths suitable for all types of glass. It is available only in specialist stained glass shops. Copper foil can also be used in a similar fashion to imitation lead.

PATINAS

Patinas are chemical solutions used to 'blacken' the copper foil to give it an authentic stained glass look. These are available from most stained glass suppliers.

FROSTING OR ETCHING MEDIUM

Sandblasting is the technique of removing or abrading a glass surface. The process of sandblasting is similar to spray painting, except that colour is removed rather than added onto the glass or mirror. This creates an etched surface which gives a frosted appearance to the glass. Etching cream or frosting paint can be used to create a frosted glass look which closely resembles professional sandblasting. Etching cream is available from specialist stained glass material suppliers. Recently, water-based frosting creams, paints and sprays have become available. These are similar to glass paints and they imitate the original decorative art of frosting.

VARNISH

Varnish is a protective layer applied to paintings to preserve them from atmospheric pollution. Since varnish stands between a painting and the outside world, with the passage of time, it accumulates dirt, and may crack and eventually discolour or lose its clarity. Glass paints themselves are lacquers or varnishes and hence need not be coated with varnish, but this extra layer will give the painting some extra protection.

If you do want to varnish the painted products, you must use a varnish that is compatible with the paints used and is recommended by the manufacturer. Most glass paint manufacturers include a varnish in their range of paints.

SUPPORTS

All paintings are carried by a support and it is the object onto which they are painted. Its function is to provide a solid durable, and stable surface onto which paint can be applied. Size, weight and cost are also relevant factors, as is compatibility with the paints. All supports have to be appropriately prepared before painting on them. They must be non-absorbent, free of dust particles, grease and residue.

Since glass paints are transparent, the best supports are acetate sheets and glass. Acetate sheets are widely available and they make an ideal surface on which to start painting. Thin acetate sheets are

available in art and craft shops and can be used to make cards, mobiles, fridge magnets and other small decorative and fun items. The ideal thickness of the acetate for making mobiles, cards and so on is 25 microns. Thicker plastic sheets obtained from DIY shops are suitable for window panels and lamps. Like glass, these have to be first cut into shape before painting on them. Some solvent-based paints react with the acetate, therefore it is best to experiment before proceeding with a project.

Any type of glass is suitable for painting on, but the best results can be seen on clear glass. Start by painting on flat pieces of glass before moving on to curved surfaces like vases and bottles. Frosted glass, coloured glass, glass with designs on it, cut glass, different types of objects made with plastic and most acrylic products are suitable for glass painting. However, the flow of the paints is the best on smooth glass and clear painted glass looks the most effective. You can paint on jam jars, vases, old bottles, and any other glassware that you would like to revamp. China, mirrors, mirror tiles, coloured glass, vases and pot pourri holders are all also suitable for painting. Tins, wooden furniture, metal objects, stones and shells can also be decorated with the outliner tubes and paints.

PALETTES

Any old saucer, jam jar lids or small aluminium foil cups are suitable for mixing the paints. I find the caps of the old paint bottles ideal for pouring small quantities of paint into, and for mixing colours. Craft shops stock a wide variety of palettes and the choice is yours. However, the paints tend to dry very quickly and plastic palettes ruin easily; also, some solvent-based paints react with plastic palettes. Ideally use a ceramic palette or small aluminium cups which are not only cheap, but disposable as well, thus saving time on washing up, so these are not recommended. If buying a ceramic palette, choose one with four to five sections, and one which has deeper grooves in it rather than the flatter ones.

ACCESSORIES

Most accessories you will need are general, household equipment with only a few items needing to be obtained from a craft or DIY shop. Masking tape, double-sided tape, pencils and eraser, scissors, cotton buds, craft knife and scalpel, vinyl resist, a hair dryer, tracing paper, plain paper, kitchen towels and tissues are the accessories which you will need for the projects. You may also need tailor's carbon paper, thread, blank greetings cards and self-adhesive vinyl-backed paper. Glass gem stones, decorative pieces of mirrors and glass, craft foil and leaf metal are some of the accessories used to decorate the paintings.

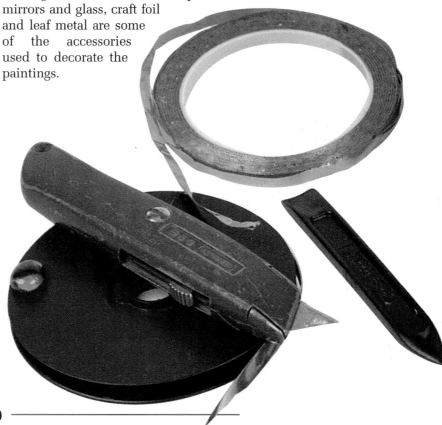

3 Colour and Design

COLOUR

Colour is a phenomenon which is perceived when light of different wavelengths is received by the eye. The colour we see usually results from the pigment. A blue sky in a painting seen in white light results from the fact that the pigments absorb all the other colour elements except the blue. Glass presents problems because it not only gives the colour sensation in a similar way to that in painting, but it also deals with light which is transmitted through the material or reflected from small particles in it.

Colour is the primary consideration in the design and use of stained glass. There are colours that dominate and absorb space, colours that soothe or excite, colours that are strong or dynamic. Colours will affect the ambience of a home and are unavoidable statements of the emotional balance of that home. Colours can describe state of mind – feeling blue today, or green with envy or in a black mood are familiar metaphors.

Look at the great examples of glass art and learn from their colour combinations. Experiment on acetate sheet or pieces of glass before making a decision. It is the personal use of colour that catches our eye and makes an object a joy to live with.

When it comes to applying colour to a design it is reassuring to discover that you do not need to master any colour theories or study great tomes. Always be prepared to place colours and textures together to see for yourself the effects. Working with colour is not an intellectual game. You should see what the heart feels, that way you will stumble across more and more personal excitement in your work. The balancing and juggling of cool colours and warm ones in design is something one learns quickly.

Simple Colour Mixing

To begin to understand colour we must appreciate that there are only three true colours: red, yellow and blue. These are called primary colours and with them we can make any other colour, except white which is not actually a colour. If we set out the three primary colours in a triangle, one at the top and two at the base, in any order and we mix adjacent colours, we have the three secondary colours: orange, green and violet, which we place in between the primary colours. By mixing any two secondary colours together, you get the tertiary colours. In addition, you have tones and tints of colours.

The colour chart is ideal when you do not want to spend a great deal of money on a whole range of colours. But if you are regularly painting it is more economical to buy a range of the shades because of the consistency of the colours.

A few tips on colour mixing are as follows:

◆ one part of red to three parts of yellow gives orange;

◆ one part of green to three parts of red gives brown;

◆ one part of red to three parts of blue gives purple;

◆ one part of blue to three parts of yellow gives olive green;

◆ one part of green to three parts of yellow gives leaf green;

◆ two parts of green to three parts of yellow gives darker green;

◆ to make darker colours add black, brown or blue;

◆ to make paler colours add colour to clear glass paint.

Adding white to any glass paint will make it opaque as white and black are the non-transparent paints.

Most glass paint ranges contain a transparent paint known as an Extender, which is a clear paint. The best way to achieve a paler shade is to add the colour of your choice to the extender. The more colour you add, the darker the paint gets. The extender works in the same way that white works in other paints.

Each individual is at liberty to choose his or her own palette, but generally the fewer the colours the more impressive the colouring is likely to be and colour mixtures should, wherever possible, be kept simple as this aids permanence and colour quality.

Select colours that suit the subject and avoid putting unnecessary colours on the palette. Try to avoid any near duplication of colours but allow for subtle variations where they are required.

Black and White

For many people, stained glass is synonymous with vibrant colours. However, restricting colours to black and white can make the transparency more pronounced. The history of the monochromatic approach can be traced back to the painted *grisaille* window which was made as early as the thirteenth century. This monochromatic approach to

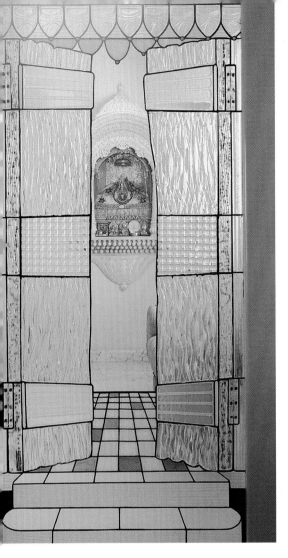

the most unlikely elements can suddenly spark each other into life. Design involves making decisions from a range of possibilities that is almost infinite.

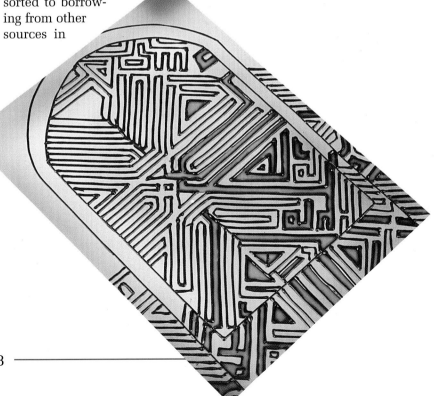

Sketch flowers, leaves or butterflies, find your favourite shapes or copy the work of admired artists and craftsmen. A motif on a little porcelain urn picked up in a junk shop, something a child has drawn with naïve charm, your favourite scarf or fabric, or something which has a particular significance for your home – all these can be transferred into a design which will make your glass painting your very own expression of craftsmanship.

Each of us has the ability to create our own personal decoration if we only relax and let our confidence grow. When designing, see how a flower would look with a vase from a painting and perhaps a border from a stained glass window. Experiment by combining them. Over the centuries, all artists have resorted to borrowing from other sources in

design has been extensively explored by stained glass artists.

Similarly, the addition of one colour can have an impact that is quite disproportionate to the actual amount of colour used. Opting for a single colour with black can be very effective. Restraint in stained glass is frequently the key to excellence.

DESIGN

Good design follows no rules and the need to remain open to the unexpected is paramount. Until you have tried a particular combination of form or colour you will not know for sure if it works because their work. Visiting card shops is a great source of inspiration, and some of my best works have been inspired by designs on cards. Sometimes you can pick a motif from a card, or sometimes the colour combination is appealing or the composition of the picture is exactly suited to your design. Similarly, books, craft fairs, art galleries and museums are also great sources of inspiration. Thanks to developments in technology and easy access to the Internet, you can 'visit' museums and art galleries all over the world.

Experiment with colours and designs, until you achieve a combination that you like. I find delicate designs work very well in glass painting, especially when the area to be filled with colour within the lead lines is small. This not only makes painting easier, it also looks beautiful.

Each project in this book is accompanied by patterns, designs and templates, with ideas or variations. But there is no need to follow all the given designs slavishly. They are there to give you a basic idea and to provide inspiration for your own designs.

Flat surfaces like acetate sheets, mirrors and glass are easier to work on.

When choosing a design for a curved or vertical object, take into consideration that the design will not lay flat against the glass. You can overcome this problem by either choosing designs which will not lose shape when placed inside the

curved surface, or by cutting the design carefully and placing it on the underside of the object and securing it properly with masking tape before proceeding.

Use the design as a guideline for tracing the pattern with the outliner. Minor deviations from the original design can add charm and individuality to the painting.

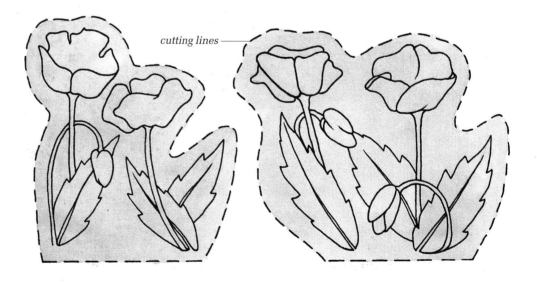

cutting lines

4 Techniques of Glass Painting

GENERAL PREPARATIONS

The surface that you are painting on should be free of dust particles and grease. Moisture, oil and chemical residues on the surface of the glass affect the durability of the paint. The paint tends to peel away if the surface is not clean, and therefore great care must be taken at this stage.

- Wash glassware in warm soapy water and remove all dust particles and grease from the surface.

- Large and bulky items like window panes can be cleaned with any commercial glass cleaning agents available in most DIY shops.

- Dry the surface to be painted thoroughly with a paper towel, before commencing to paint on it.

- Wipe acetate sheets with a moist cloth and then dry the surface with a kitchen towel.

- Paint absorbent materials like stone and wood with a coat of lacquer before painting on them.

THE OUTLINER PASTE

The outliner or cerne relief can be applied on most previously degreased transparent or opaque surfaces. It is applied directly by pressing slightly and evenly on the tube with the tip grazing the surface. The thickness of the line depends on the tip's diameter and the pressure exerted.

Practise with the outliner tube before starting your first project. The amount of pressure and steadiness determines the size and uniformity of the design. The greater the pressure, the thicker the line. Once you have understood how the outliner tube works, and have learnt to control its flow, the rest is easy.

- Some outliner tubes are already pierced while others are sealed and have to be pierced with a single-headed pin in order to release the outliner. The paste tends to ooze out of the tube initially, thus making it difficult to control the flow.

- Open the tube and place it on top of a kitchen towel. The paste will ooze out for a few seconds. It is best to wait until this has stopped before using the outliner.

◆ To begin with, place the nozzle directly on the surface, apply pressure gently and let the paste flow, moving the nozzle in a similar fashion to writing.

◆ However, if you hold the nozzle touching the glass while 'drawing' with the cerne relief, the outline is wobbly and uneven. The best way to get a smooth outline is by touching the tip of the nozzle at the point of starting the design, then apply a little pressure with your thumb, and gently lift the nozzle about a centimetre away from the surface, pulling the paste as you go along, and then touching the surface again 1.2–1.6in (3–4cm) away from the point where you started. Repeat this step until the design is complete. Guide the paste gently as you go along and with practice you will be able to hold the paste for a longer time. As you gain more control of the outliner tube you will then be able to complete the design without any 'touchdowns', thus giving a very smooth and perfect outline. Using the outliner is very similar to icing a cake and with a little practise, you will be able to use the outliner very effectively.

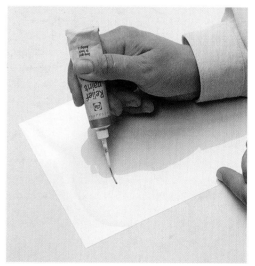

◆ The trick to controlling the flow of the outliner is to hold the tube at the top end between your thumb and forefinger. Place the nozzle at the point where you would like to start applying the cerne relief. The tube should be held at a slant of 45 degrees to the surface. Squeeze gently, raising the hand slightly to control the direction of the paste, (do not pull as this will break the thread), then ease pressure and touch down to the surface. If the

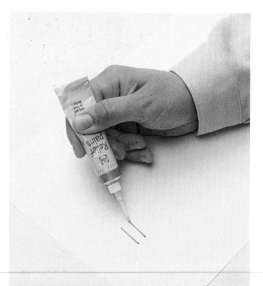

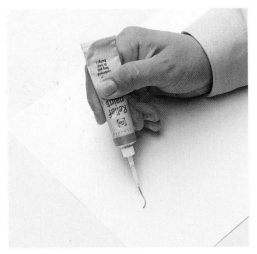

thread is allowed to touch the surface while being drawn across it will result in a crooked or broken line.

- For curved outlines, touch the tube to the surface, squeeze gently, then take the tube away from the surface, allowing the paste to fall along the lines of the pattern.

- For dots, place the point of the tube (at a 90-degree angle) against the surface, squeeze gently, stop, then lift the tube away. The size of the dots can be varied according to the amount of pressure exerted. For example, five dots in a small circle with a centre dot form a forget-me-not.

- For teardrops, pipe a series of pulled dots (holding the tube at 45 degrees) in a teardrop shape, each bulb covering the tail of the previous teardrop.

- For herringbone, hold the tube at a 45-degree angle, and pipe teardrop shapes alternately from left to right.

- For scrolls, pipe the letter 'C' joined to the tail of the previous one.

- For a thick line, touch the tip of the nozzle to the support and while applying pressure trace the design with the tube.

WATCH POINTS

- While using the outliner tube, you must remember that control of the flow of the paste depends upon the pressure applied and the amount that you drag the tube. If the pressure is too much, the outline will be thick, if the pressure is too little, the outline will be thin. Dragging the tube too slowly will result in the outline being thick and uneven, and pulling the tube too quickly will break the paste line. Achieving a balance between the amount of pressure applied and pulling the paste is the key to smooth and even lines. At first this may seem difficult, but with a little practice you will be able to achieve excellent results.

- The different makes of paste will handle in different ways. Some pastes have air bubbles in them which affect the finish of the outline. It is best to test the outliners before using them. Practise on a piece of acetate to get the feel of the tube before starting on the projects.

- Again, the overall finish of these outliners depends on the make used and it is best to use the same brand as the paint you are using, although some can be mixed. I personally prefer the outliner tubes of Royal Sovereign.

PAINT

Painting on glass is very different to painting with other media. One of my students described it as 'blobbing', and I feel the word aptly describes glass painting.

- The paints should be stirred before use.

- Fill the brush with the glass paint, taking care not to overload it. Do not tap the brush against the palette as you would while painting with any other medium. Drop a small quantity of paint (blob) on the area to be painted and push the paint with the brush until the paint covers this area. Add more paint if necessary, until the area is covered. Do not use brushstrokes. You will notice that by 'pushing' the paint to cover an area, you get a smooth and glossy finish.

- Do not paint over dried paint; completely cover each piece of design before taking a break.

- Large areas should be covered quickly using an extra amount of paint, which will allow you to spread the paint easily and reduce brushmarks. Painting on top of dried paint gives an uneven finish.

- It is better to use more paint rather than less, as the paint spreads easily and levels itself.

- If you are using the outliner first and then filling in the paint, take care that there aren't any gaps between the outliner and the paint. Hold the painted surface against the light and fill any gaps before the paint dries completely.

◆ Small detailed lines and shading can be done by painting a second coat over the first, but take care that the first coat has completely hardened before applying the second.

◆ The best way to achieve the real 'stained' glass effect is to use two shades together, applying a little bit of one colour and then adding the second colour next to it. As the paint dries, the colours intermingle, giving a marbled look to the painting. Using white with any colour in this way gives the effect of Baroque or hand-rolled glass. Similarly, black beside any colour gives some stunning results.

◆ Adding drops of thinner to any painted surface just after applying the paint will again give a beautiful hand-rolled glass effect.

ENLARGING OR REDUCING DESIGNS

Any design can be reduced or enlarged to suit your needs by using a simple grid system, pantograph or photocopier. I personally prefer using the photocopier as it is a very quick and inexpensive method of enlarging or reducing designs and is usually easily available.

A pantograph can be purchased from an art or craft shop. The device consists of four flattened rods and at the appropriate points a tracing point and a drawing point are fixed to the rods. The pantograph has hinges at the crossing points and can be adjusted to enlarge or reduce the design.

Of course, with the development of home scanners, it is possible to alter designs completely to suit your individual needs. If you have access to computers and a scanner, you can use it to make templates for glass painting.

TRANSFERRING DESIGNS

When I first started glass painting, I used to transfer designs by tracing onto the glass, using carbon paper or by drawing directly onto the glassware with pens suitable for glass painting. The problem with this method is that the pencil lines can be seen through the paint, giving a very amateurish look to the decoration.

Over the years, I have realized that the best way to transfer a design is to enlarge or reduce it in proportion to the support, then, using masking tape, secure it underneath the object. Supports like wood or vases and bottles in which the design cannot be inserted are best decorated with abstract or freehand designs.

HOW TO BEGIN

Be realistic about your first attempts. Begin with something small and with a simple design to guarantee successful results. As your confidence grows, you will be able to tackle some of the more complicated designs. Make sure that you have everything you will require to hand before beginning any project. As explained in the chapter on MATERIALS AND EQUIPMENT, you need not make a large initial outlay on tools or materials. Keep to a few basic colours for your first project, and add to your range as you progress.

glass vase

template of design

masking tape

5 Step-by-Step

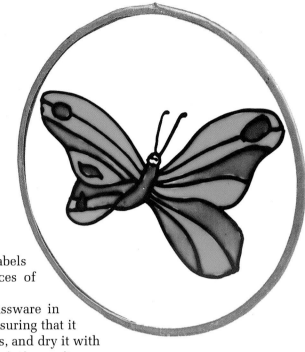

PREPARATION

Step 1. Choose the design, and enlarge or reduce it on a photocopier, as per requirement.

Step 2. Cut the design 1cm away from the outline. This makes it easier to fix onto the glassware.

cutting lines

Your template is now ready.

GETTING STARTED

Step 1. Protect your clothes with an apron or old shirt, and cover your work surface with an old cloth or papers. Your work surface should be at a comfortable height, and should be clear of anything other than the items you are going to need when painting.

Step 2. The surface you are painting on must be free of dust particles and grease.

Step 3. Peel off any labels and clean off all traces of adhesive.

Step 4. Wash the glassware in warm soapy water, ensuring that it is free of dust particles, and dry it with a paper towel before painting on it.

Step 5. Wipe off all water marks before you start painting, and clean off any finger marks with the paper towel.

STEP-BY-STEP

There are primarily two methods of glass painting:

The First Method of Glass Painting: Paint First, Outliner Second

The first method of painting on glass is mainly suitable for flat surfaces and is ideal for a beginner. This method gives you the feel of the paints and the outliner.

Step 1. Place the acetate or glass that is to be painted over the design, using masking tape to hold it in place.

Step 2. Start your work from the top to avoid accidental smudges.

Step 3. Pour a little paint into the mixing palette. Using the brush, dribble a few drops of paint onto the surface of the area to be painted.

The paint will flow easily and fill the area. Follow the general instructions described in PAINT (Chapter 4), taking care to contain the paint within the design.

Step 4. If the paint accidentally spills or spreads, wipe it immediately with a soft moist cloth or tissue.

Step 5. Paint in one colour at a time.

Step 6. It is advisable to let one colour dry before using the next colour as they may run into each other. Take care to clean the brush thoroughly between colours.

Step 7. When the paint is dry, trace the outline of the design, following the pattern, by lightly squeezing the tube. Follow the general instructions described in OUTLINER PASTE (Chapter 4).

Step 8. Wipe any blobs of outliner paste onto a tissue before continuing with the outline on the painting.

Step 9. If there is an accident with the outliner, clean it immediately with a moist cloth or let it dry overnight and then scrape it off carefully with a craft knife.

Step 10. The outliner paste takes approximately half an hour or so to dry, but leave it overnight before handling it further.

Method Two: Outliner First, Paint Second

This method is suitable for all types of projects and for all types of surfaces.

Step 1. Place the design in position, under the surface to be painted, using masking tape to hold it in place.

Step 2. Lay the object to be painted horizontally on the work surface. Start your work from the top to avoid accidental smudges.

Step 3. Trace the outline of the design with the outliner tube, following the pattern by lightly squeezing the outliner paste, until you have covered the whole design.

Step 4. Follow the instructions in the section on OUTLINER PASTE (Chapter 4) while tracing the design. Wipe blobs of outliner paste onto a tissue before continuing with the outline on the surface, as this will help to give a neat finish.

Step 5. Let the outliner dry for approximately an hour or so before filling in the paint. The contour paste is raised against the surface and creates separate areas within the design. In case of an accident with the outliner tube, clean it immediately with a moist cloth or let it dry overnight and then scrape it off carefully with a craft knife.

Step 6. Pour a few drops of paint into the mixing palette. Using the brush, drop the paint into the areas within the design, filling it with paint. Spread the paint by using the brush to cover the area. The paint spreads easily to the outliner paste lines.

Step 7. The paint will spread easily and the outliner paste will hold the colour separately, giving the appearance of individual pieces of glass. The paint takes approximately ten to fifteen minutes to dry partially but about a day to harden.

Step 8. Follow the instructions in the section on PAINT (Chapter 4) to fill in the colours.

Step 9. If the paint accidentally spills or spreads, wipe it immediately with a soft moist cloth or tissue and it will come clean.

Step 13. If you accidentally paint over the outliner, touch the painted area with the outliner, covering the mistake.

Step 14. Once all areas have been painted your object is ready.

VARNISHING

Glass paints are lacquer-based and so do not require varnishing. However, a coat of varnish will protect the painting, so you may choose to varnish a painted object.

The surface to be varnished must be absolutely dry, otherwise the varnish will pick up and damage the painting. Ensure that the work to be varnished is clean. Specks of dust and other unwanted particles can appear from nowhere, so gently brush the surface with a clean soft rag or soft brush prior to varnishing.

Always varnish in a clear atmosphere. Once grit or dust gets into the varnish it is difficult to remove it without damaging the paint. Varnishing must not be done in haste. Take your time with this aspect of painting.

Some varnishes react with the paints, and the paints may discolour or peel away. It is essential you experiment on a small piece of glass before using any combination of paint and varnish. Using the manufacturer's recommended varnish is always advisable.

Step 10. Paint in one colour at a time.

Step 11. It is advisable to let one colour dry before using the second colour as they may run into each other. Take care to clean the brush thoroughly between colours.

Step 12. Occasionally lift the object to check that the colour is even and has spread to the edges. Take precautions when lifting the painted object, because the wet paint tends to drip. Touch the gaps between the paint and the outliner immediately.

Varnishing can be carried out with an undiluted medium straight from the bottle or by pouring a little medium into a clean saucer. Always varnish with a soft brush as hard brushes leave brushstrokes, which will look unsightly. Clean brushes immediately after varnishing. Dried varnish is very hard to remove and may harm the brush.

To be quite certain of completely covering the surface with varnish, look obliquely along the work. Any untouched areas will be detected immediately because of the reflected light.

WATCH POINTS

- The paints and the outliners are both air-drying products. Always keep the paint bottle closed because as soon as the paint is exposed to air, the paint will get thick and gummy and eventually dry out.

- You can thin the paint by using the recommended thinner if it is solvent-based, and water if it is water-based.

- Some paints can be thinned with ordinary white spirit, but it is advisable to thin the paints with the manufacturer's recommended thinner.

- Always work from top to bottom to avoid accidental smudges.

- The greatest advantage with glass painting is that accidental spills or spreads of paint can be corrected by wiping the error immediately with a moist cloth or cotton bud.

- Similarly, accidental smudges of the outliner can be wiped with a moist cloth or cotton bud. Alternatively, let the paste dry overnight and then scrape it off carefully with a craft knife.

- You can speed the process of drying by using a hairdryer, but ideally let the paints and outliner dry naturally.

- As you get more and more confident with glass painting, you can start painting two or three items at the same time, thus economizing on time as well as paints and the outliner.

- Round objects are slightly more tricky. Any project with a double curvature will need tucks cut into the design to make it lie flat against the glass. This must be taken into consideration as some of the design may be lost in the tucks. Try out your design carefully for fit before starting.

- Test ways of placing the item at a good angle to work with, so that it will not move and is also easy to handle.

- It is better to start painting on clear glass before moving on to frosted and opaque glass as the patterns can be seen clearly through the clear glass.

CARE OF PAINTED GLASSWARE

- Painted glassware can be washed in cold soapy water, but do not use abrasives.

- Wipe over gently and carefully and never soak any painted surface in water.

- Fingerprints can be cleaned with a soft moist cloth.

- Allow plenty of time for the paint to harden off.

- Some glass paints are fade resistant and these will be suitable for projects exposed to sunlight.

- As glass paints are lacquer-based they attract dust very easily. Also if pressure is applied to the painted surface, it marks easily. Preferably pack all painted glassware in individual cartons. If the glassware is wrapped in bubblewrap or tissue paper for a long period of time, the paper tends to stick to the paints.

◆ Varnishing the painted objects protects them from knocks and scratches.

◆ With proper care and protection painted glass objects will give years of pleasure. When painting a surface exposed to the elements, the best way to protect the paint is to seal it between two layers of glass, and this will then last for many years without being damaged.

STARTING ALL OVER AGAIN

Every artist at some point will be unhappy with their finished work. There might be various reasons for the dissatisfaction. You are probably not happy with colour combination or design or the overall image that the finished object is conveying. In such a situation, you can restart the decoration. All you have to do is to soak the decorated glassware in warm water. The paint as well the outliner paste will peel away after a few hours. Wash and scrub any residues of paint or outliner paste. Dry the object, and you can start decorating it all over again!

The paint and the outliner can also be removed using white spirit or the manufacturer's recommended thinner, but this method is comparatively more expensive and time-consuming than soaking in warm water.

PROJECT 1: LAMP

USING ONLY AN OUTLINER TUBE TO DECORATE COLOURED GLASS

Decorating coloured glass and understanding the control of the outliner tube.

This simple project introduces a glass painter to the outliner tube. It is an easy way to learn to control the outliner tube without any wastage.

There is a wide range of coloured glassware available in the shops. Most of these are cheap and cheerful, and make excellent decorative items for the home or as gifts.

In this project I have decorated a simple coloured candle holder with Gold cerne relief. This project will help you to overcome the fear of handling an outliner tube. By the time you have completed this simple project, you will have gained considerable control over the outliner, and will understand how to control the flow of the outliner paste.

MATERIALS

◆ Coloured glass lamp

◆ Gold outliner tube

ACCESSORIES

◆ Cotton buds

◆ Paper towel

◆ Craft knife

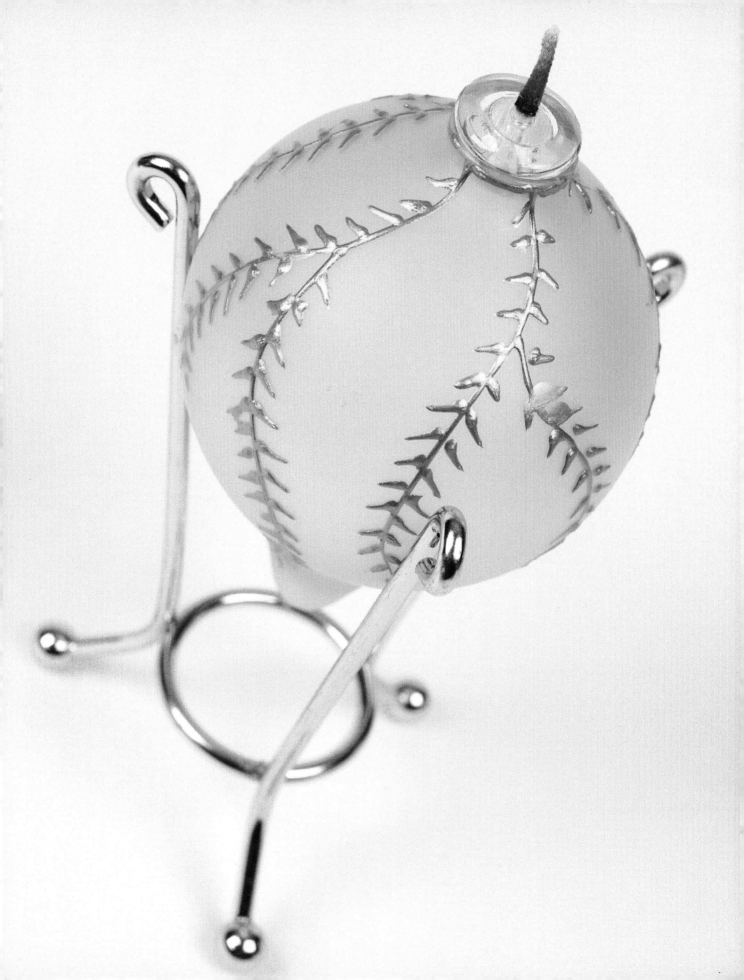

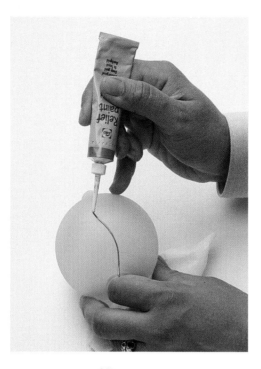

to hold the paste for a longer time. As you gain more control of the outliner tube you will then be able to complete the design without any 'touchdowns', thus giving a smooth and perfect outline.

Step 6. The tube should be held at a slant of 45 degrees to the surface. Squeeze gently, raising the hand slightly to control the direction of the paste, (do not pull as this will break the thread), then ease pressure and touch down to the surface.

Step 7. For curved outlines, touch the tube to the surface, squeeze gently, then take the tube away from the surface, allowing the paste to fall in a random design.

TIP:

The trick to controlling the flow of the outliner is to hold the tube at the top end between your thumb and forefinger. Place the nozzle at the point where you would like to start applying the cerne relief.

STEP-BY-STEP INSTRUCTIONS

Step 1. Protect your clothes with an apron or an old shirt, and cover your work surface with an old cloth or papers.

Step 2. Wash the candle holder in warm soapy water, ensuring that it is free of dust particles, and dry it with a kitchen towel before painting on it.

Step 3. Open the tube and place it on top of a kitchen towel. The paste will ooze out for a few seconds. Start using the tube after the paste has stopped oozing out.

Step 4. Touch the tip of the nozzle at the point of starting the design, then apply a little pressure with your thumb, and gently lift the nozzle about a centimetre away from the surface, pulling the paste as you go along, and then touching the surface at approximately 3cm away from the point where you started. Repeat this step until the design is complete.

Step 5. Guide the paste gently as you go along and with practice you will be able

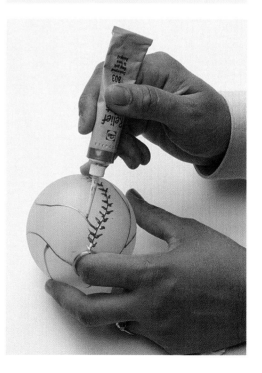

Step 8. Once you have completed the 'vine' design all over the lamp, fill in the leaves by holding the tube at a 45-degree angle and piping teardrop shapes alternately from left to right.

Step 9. Once you have decorated the glass your project is complete. Let it dry overnight before handling it.

WATCH POINTS

◆ While using the outliner tube you must remember that control of the flow of the paste depends on the pressure applied and the amount that you drag the tube.

◆ The different makes of paste will handle in different ways. Some pastes have air bubbles in them which affect the finish of the outline. It is best to test the outliners before using them. Practise on a piece of acetate to get the feel of the tube before starting on the project.

PROJECT 2: MAKING A MOBILE USING BLACK OUTLINER

AN ALPHABET MOBILE

*Decorating flat surfaces
and painting on acetate sheets.*

This craft is perhaps not very accurately described as 'Glass' painting, as the paints are very versatile and can be used on almost any nonporous surface. However, as the paints are transparent their true potential is

achieved when they are painted on a surface which allows light to pass through it.

Acetate sheets or perspex are plastic materials which are transparent, unbreakable and easily available. They are relatively inexpensive and the best thing about them is that they can be cut into shapes very easily. Painting on a flat surface is easier than painting on a vertical surface. The ideal thickness for the acetate sheet should be 25 microns. You can paint on any thickness of acetate, but if the sheet is too thin, it tends to curl at the edges when painted, and if it is too thick, it is not easy to cut. Acetate sheets are available in different colours, but clear is ideal for painting.

In this project, we make and paint a mobile, which will both introduce a child to the alphabet and you to the art of painting on 'glass'.

MATERIALS

- Six A5 clear acetate sheets of 25 microns thickness

- Black outliner tube

- Transparent water-based glass paints (red, blue, green and yellow)

- No. 2 synthetic or fine hair watercolour brush

ACCESSORIES

- Template of the designs

- Scissors

- Masking tape

- Sewing thread

- Hole punch

- Cotton buds

- Paper towel

See PREPARATION and GETTING STARTED earlier in this chapter.

STEP-BY-STEP INSTRUCTIONS

Step 1. Place the acetate sheet on top of the design and hold it in place with masking tape.

TIP:

Start your work from the top to avoid accidental smudges.

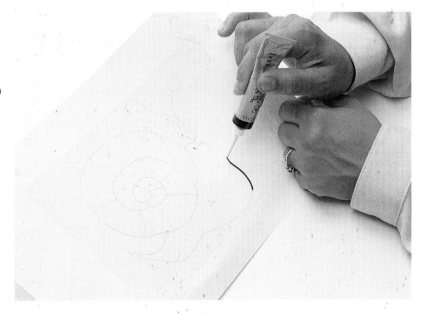

TIP:

Wipe blobs of outliner paste onto a tissue before continuing with the outline on the painting, as this will help to give a very neat finish.

Step 2. Trace the outline of the designs with the black outliner tube, following the pattern by lightly squeezing the outliner paste, until you have covered the whole design.

TIP:

If there is an accident with the outliner, clean it immediately with a moist cloth or let it dry overnight and then scrape it off carefully with a craft knife.

Step 3. Trace all the designs onto the acetate sheets and let them dry.

Step 4. Let the outliner dry for approximately an hour or so before filling in the paint. The outliner lines are raised against the surface and create separate areas within the design.

Step 5. Pour a few drops of red paint into the mixing palette. Using the brush, drop the paint into the 'face' of the snail, filling it with paint. Spread the paint by using the brush to cover the area.

Step 6. The paint will spread easily and the outliner paste will hold the colour separately. The paint takes approximately 10 to 15 minutes to dry partially but about a day to harden.

Step 7. Clean the brush thoroughly with water, and then pour some blue paint into the palette. Add a few drops of yellow paint and stir thoroughly. You will get

TIP:

If the paint accidentally spills or spreads, wipe it immediately with a soft moist cloth or tissue and it will come clean.

a dark green colour. Use this to colour parts of the snail.

Step 8. As you add more yellow the shade of green will become paler. You can then colour in the rest of the snail with the different shades of green.

Step 9. When you have painted the snail, lift the acetate sheet to check that the colour is even and has spread to the edges and that there are no unpainted areas.

Step 10. Once all areas have been covered your snail is ready. Let it dry for a few hours before handling it.

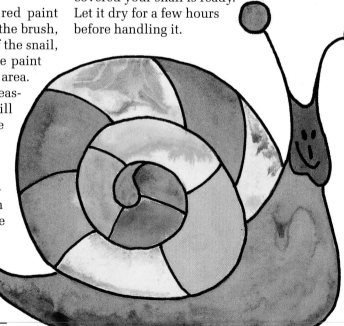

Step 11. Continue in a similar way filling each design with colours of your choice.

Making the Mobile

Step 1. Once the paint is dry, cut along the outline of the acetate allowing ½in (1.2cm) space both at the top and the bottom of the design for making a hole with the hole punch.
Step 2. Tie lengths of string to attach the pieces to make the mobile.
Step 3. Add a longer piece of string to the top of the snail.

The mobile is ready.

Acetate sheets are very versatile, easy to decorate and great fun for all the family.

Some of the other things you can make by painting and cutting acetate sheets are suncatchers, Christmas tree decorations, fridge magnets, earrings, brooches and pendants.

PROJECT 3: GREETING CARD

CREATING A ROSE DESIGN USING A GOLD OUTLINER TUBE

Using the first method of glass painting where the outliner is applied after the design has been painted.

The special quality of handmade cards lies in their originality, and making them is as much fun as receiving them. Blank cards with oval, square or rectangular apertures are available in craft shops, in various sizes. These can be used as greeting cards, invitations, gift tags and so on.

Here I have chosen a rose design and in this project you are introduced to the technique of painting first and then finishing with the outliner. This technique works very well on flat surfaces and especially when using gold outliner tubes. The advantage of this technique is that it gives a very neat finish. The project can be completed in a few hours.

MATERIALS

◆ One A5 acetate sheet of 25 microns thickness

◆ One card and envelope

◆ Transparent water-based glass paints (crimson and green)

◆ Gold outliner tube

◆ No. 2 synthetic watercolour brush

ACCESSORIES

◆ Template of design

◆ Scissors

◆ Masking tape

◆ Double-sided tape

◆ Cotton buds

◆ Paper towel

◆ Craft knife

See PREPARATION and GETTING STARTED earlier in this chapter.

STEP-BY-STEP INSTRUCTIONS

Step 1. Wipe the acetate sheet with a piece of kitchen towel, taking care that it is free of dust particles.
Step 2. Enlarge or reduce design according to requirements.
Step 3. Place the sheet over the design, using the masking tape to hold it in place.
Step 4. Pour a few drops of paint into the mixing palette. Using the brush,

apply a few drops of paint at a time to the area to be painted. It will spread easily with a little help from the brush.

Step 5. Paint in all the areas that need to be covered with the red paint.

Step 6. Let it dry for at least half an hour or so. Once the paint is dry, pour some green paint into the palette. Follow steps three and four, painting in the 'leaf' areas.

Step 7. Let the paint dry for a few hours.

Step 8. Since the paint is transparent, you can still see the design through the colour. When completely dry, trace the design with the gold outliner. This gives an intricate finish to the design.

Step 9. Leave the outliner for a few hours to dry.

Step 10. Your design is now ready to be mounted in a card of your choice.

Step 11. Place the aperture of the card over your design and then carefully turn everything over. Using double-sided tape, carefully stick the acetate to the card, fold over the extra flap and stick in position.

Your card is ready.

You can make gift tags, invitations, bookmarks, place-cards and nameplates in a similar way. When a painted acetate sheet is stuck onto a piece of white card, the colours are altered dramatically and appear brighter.

PROJECT 4: SUN CATCHER

BUTTERFLY DESIGN

Decorating a flat piece of glass by tracing the outline of the design with the cerne relief and then filling it in with paint.

A suncatcher decorated with glass paints is an ideal way to decorate your window. This is an easy project and will liven up any window. It also provides you with practice at painting on glass and controlling the outliner. The project can be completed in a day and is ideal for a beginner.

MATERIALS

◆ Ready leaded 6in (15cm) diameter glass roundel

◆ Transparent water-based or solvent-based glass paints (turquoise and light green)

- Black outliner tube

- No. 2 synthetic watercolour brush

- Self-adhesive hook

ACCESSORIES

- Template of design

- Scissors

- Masking tape

- Cotton buds

- Paper towel

- Craft knife

- Cold soapy water

See PREPARATION and GETTING STARTED earlier in this chapter.

STEP-BY-STEP INSTRUCTIONS

Step 1. Place the glass roundel on top of the design and hold it in place with masking tape.

Step 2. Trace the outline of the designs with the black outliner tube, following the pattern by lightly squeezing the outliner paste, until you have covered the whole design.

TIP:

Start your work from the top to avoid accidental smudges.

TIP:

Wipe blobs of outliner paste onto a tissue before continuing with the outline on the painting, as this will help to give a very neat finish.

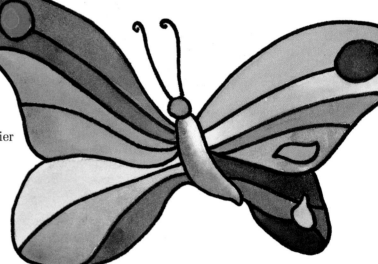

Step 3. Let the outliner dry for approximately an hour or so before filling in the paint. The outliner lines are raised against the surface and create separate areas within the design.

TIP:

If there is an accident with the outliner, clean it immediately with a moist cloth or let it dry overnight and then scrape it off carefully with a craft knife.

Step 4. Pour a few drops of green paint into the mixing palette. Using the brush, drop the paint into the 'green' areas of the butterfly, filling it with paint. Spread the paint by using the brush to cover the area.

Step 5. The paint will spread out easily and the outliner paste will hold the colour separately. The paint will take approximately ten to fifteen minutes to dry partially, but about a day to harden fully.

Step 6. Clean the brush thoroughly (with water if using water-based paints

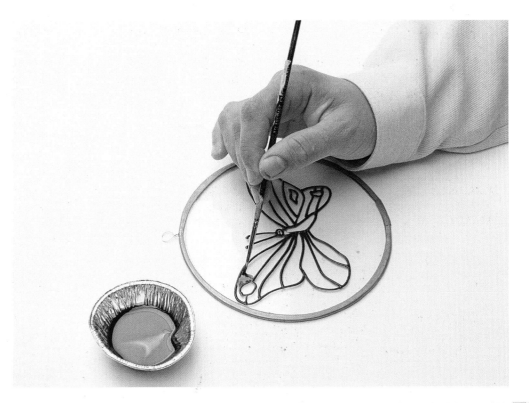

and with a brush cleaner if you are using solvent-based paints), and then pour some turquoise paint into the palette. Fill in the 'turquoise' areas with the paint following steps 4 and 5.

Step 7. Once all the areas have been covered, your suncatcher is ready to use. Let it dry for a few hours before handling it.

Step 8. Use the self-adhesive hook to hang it in any window.

See CARE OF PAINTED GLASSWARE earlier in this chapter.

PROJECT 5: WINE GLASSES

GEOMETRIC DESIGN

Decorating wine glasses in a geometric design and using only black and white paints to decorate them.

The range of glassware that is available is unlimited, and decorating any glass is very enjoyable. Using simple patterns and restricting the use of colour to black and white can be very effective. Instead of painting identical designs on a set of glasses, you can vary the design, following the basic theme. This makes painting fun and adds individuality to each glass.

MATERIALS

- Four wine glasses

- Transparent solvent-based glass paints (black and white)

- Black outliner tube

- No. 2 synthetic watercolour brush

ACCESSORIES

- Template of design

- Scissors

- Masking tape

TIP:

Wipe blobs of outliner paste onto a tissue before continuing with the outline on the painting, as this will help to give a neat finish.

- Cotton buds

- Paper towel

- Craft knife

- Cold soapy water

See PREPARATION and GETTING STARTED earlier in this chapter.

STEP-BY-STEP INSTRUCTIONS

Step 1. Place the template in position, under the surface to be painted. Use masking tape to hold it in place.
Step 2. Hold the glass horizontally on the work surface. Prop it up to ensure it doesn't move whilst you are painting.
Step 3. Trace the outline of the designs with the black outliner tube, following the pattern by lightly squeezing the outliner paste, until you have covered the design on one side of the glass. Leave to dry for at least 15 to 20 minutes, before proceeding with the other side.

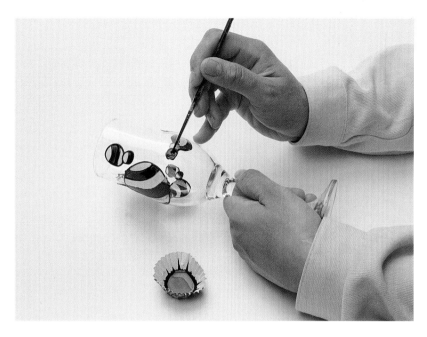

TIP:

To save time, you can paint one side of all the glasses first, and then proceed with the other side, allowing 15 to 20 minutes for the paint to dry.

'black' areas with the paint following steps four and five.

Step 8. The black and white paints are opaque. An interesting pattern is created if you leave some areas unpainted. Follow a random pattern of filling in some areas, while leaving others unpainted.

Note: Glass paints are suitable for decorative purposes only and it is not advisable to paint around the rim of glasses, if the glasses are to be used for drinking purposes.

Also take care not to paint on any areas where food will touch the paint.

See CARE OF PAINTED GLASSWARE earlier in this chapter.

PROJECT 6: DECORATING A VASE

IRIS DESIGN USING SILVER OUTLINE

Decorating a vertical and curved surface by tracing the outline of the design with the cerne relief and then filling it in with paint.

TIP:

If there is an accident with the outliner, clean it immediately with a moist cloth or let it dry overnight and then scrape it off carefully with a craft knife.

Step 4. Let the outliner dry for approximately an hour or so before filling in the paint. The outliner lines are raised against the surface and create separate areas within the design.

Step 5. Pour a few drops of 'white' paint into the mixing palette. Using the brush, drop the paint into the 'white' areas of the design, filling it with paint. Spread the paint by using the brush to cover the area.

Step 6. The paint will spread easily and the outliner paste will hold the colour separately. The paint takes approximately 10 to 15 minutes to dry partially but about a day to harden.

TIP:

If the paint accidentally spills or spreads, wipe it immediately with a soft moist cloth or tissue and it will come clean.

Step 7. Clean the brush thoroughly with the brush cleaner, and then pour some black paint into the palette. Fill in the

P ainting on vertical surfaces is a little more tricky than painting on flat surfaces. In this project, you will learn to deal with the problems that

TIP:

Start your work from the top to avoid accidental smudges.

arise within painting on vertical objects. The advantage of first painting on small objects like glasses and mini vases is that you begin to understand the flow of the paint and the best way of controlling it.

MATERIALS

◆ One 10in (25cm) tall glass

◆ Transparent glass paints (green and light blue)

◆ Extender

◆ Silver outliner tube

◆ No. 2 nylon or fine hair water-colour brush

ACCESSORIES

◆ Template of design

◆ Scissors

◆ Masking Tape

◆ Cotton buds

◆ Paper towel

◆ Craft knife

◆ Cold soapy water

See PREPARATION and GETTING STARTED earlier in this chapter.

STEP-BY-STEP INSTRUCTIONS

Step 1. Place the design in position, under the surface to be painted, using masking tape to hold it in place.

Step 2. Lay the vase to be painted down horizontally on the work surface. Prop it up to ensure it doesn't move whilst you are painting.

Step 3. Trace the outline of the design with the silver outliner tube, following the pattern by lightly squeezing the outliner paste, until you have covered the whole design.

Step 4. Let the outliner dry for approximately half an hour or so.

TIP:

Wipe blobs of outliner paste onto a tissue before continuing with the outline as this will help to give a neat finish.

Step 5. After cleaning any blobs away, let the outliner dry for another hour or so before filling in the paint. The outliner lines are raised against the surface and create separate areas within the design.

Step 6. Pour a few drops of blue paint into the palette and add a few drops of the extender to the paint. Do not mix the two, but let them merge into each other in the palette.

TIP:

If there is an accident with the outliner, clean it immediately with a moist cloth. Alternatively, let it dry overnight and then scrape it off carefully with a craft knife. If you have made a minor mistake it is advisable to wipe it off immediately.

Step 7. Using the brush, drop the paint into the 'petal' areas within the design.

TIP:

If the brush is overloaded with paint, some of it will trickle down the side. Wipe it immediately with a cotton bud, taking care not to smudge any other area of the painting.

Step 8. When taking the paint from the palette alternate between the blue colour and the extender. By doing this, you get a shaded effect on the petals rather than a flat colour.

Step 9. The paint will spread easily and the outliner paste will hold the colour separately, giving the appearance of individual pieces of glass. The paint takes approximately 10 to 15 minutes to dry partially but about a day to harden.

Step 10. Clean the brush thoroughly with the brush cleaner, and then pour some light green paint into the palette and fill in the 'leaf' areas with the paint.

Step 11. Lift the object now and then to check that the colour is even and has spread to the edges and that there are no unpainted gaps.

Step 12. Once all areas have been covered your vase is ready. Leave it to dry before handling it.

Similar designs and techniques can be used to decorate glasses, bottles, etc.

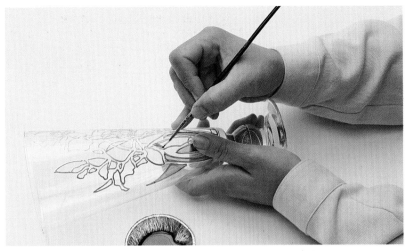

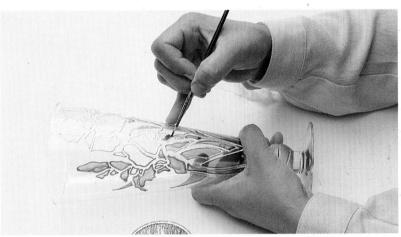

TIP:

If the paint accidentally spills or spreads, wipe it immediately with a moist cotton bud or tissue and it will come clean.

Note: Glass paints are suitable for decorative purposes only and it is not advisable to paint around the rim of glasses, if they are to be used for drinking purposes. Also take care not to paint on any areas where food will touch the paint.

See CARE OF PAINTED GLASSWARE earlier in this chapter.

TIP:

If you accidentally paint over the outliner, touch the painted area with the outliner covering the error.

PROJECT 7: POPPY VASE

CREATING A POPPY DESIGN USING GOLD OUTLINER

Decorating a clear vase by mixing the paints directly on the vase instead of mixing in a palette.

Poppies are very simple to create but at the same time are very attractive. I have used poppies in many of my projects and I do a whole range of poppy designs for my painted glassware range. These have always been bestsellers over the years.

Once you have painted one vertical object you will realize how simple it is to paint others. This project will introduce you to mixing paints directly on the vase itself. The effect of this colour mixing is quite stunning, because you get different shades as the colours mingle with each other. As the yellow mixes with the red, the petal will have shades ranging from a pale orange to a bright red, without much effort. I really enjoy painting in this manner because each vase is then a unique creation.

Any design can be used for glass painting, but if you are painting a vertical or curved surface, and the area to be painted within the outline is more than about 1in (2.5cm) wide, the paint tends to have an uneven finish, and brushmarks will be visible. For an effective design, choose a pattern with this in mind.

MATERIALS

- One clear glass vase

- Transparent glass paints (crimson, light green and yellow)

- Gold outliner tube

- No. 2 synthetic or fine hair water-colour brush

ACCESSORIES

- Template of design

- Scissors

- Masking tape

- Cotton buds

- Paper towel

- Craft knife

See PREPARATION and GETTING STARTED earlier in this chapter.

STEP-BY-STEP INSTRUCTIONS

Step 1. Place the design in position, under the surface to be painted, using masking tape to hold it in place.

TIP:

Start your work from the top to avoid accidental smudges.

TIP:

Wipe blobs of outliner paste onto a tissue before continuing with the outline on the painting.

Step 2. Lay the vase to be painted horizontally on the work surface. Prop it up to ensure it doesn't move whilst you are painting.

Step 3. Trace the outline of the design with the gold outliner tube, following the pattern by lightly squeezing the outliner paste, until you have covered the whole design.

Step 4. You do not have to follow the pattern slavishly and if there is a slight difference in the pattern size or shape, it doesn't matter.

Step 5. Only trace the outline of the flowers and leaves. Do not trace the inside stamens of the flowers and veins of the leaves.

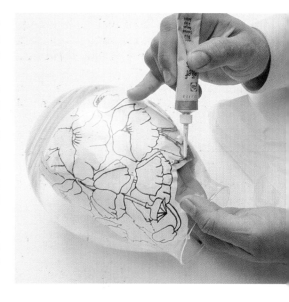

TIP:

If there is an accident with the outliner, clean it immediately with a moist cotton bud, or let it dry overnight and then scrape it off carefully with a craft knife.

Step 6. Let the outliner dry for approximately an hour or so before filling in the paint. The outliner lines are raised against the surface and create separate areas within the design.

TIP:

If the paint accidentally spills or spreads, wipe it immediately with a soft moist cloth or tissue and it will come clean.

Step 7. Pour a few drops of green paint into the mixing palette. Using the brush, drop the paint into the 'leaf' areas within the design, filling them with paint. Spread the paint by using the brush to cover the area. The paint spreads easily to the outliner paste lines.

Step 8. The paint will spread easily and the outliner paste will hold the colour separately, giving the appearance of individual pieces of glass. The paint takes approximately 10 to 15 minutes to dry partially but about a day to harden.

Step 9. While painting the leaves, occasionally lift the vase and hold it against the light to see if there are any gaps between the paint and the outliner. These gaps can either be touched up with the paint or with the outliner.

Step 10. Clean the brush thoroughly, and then pour some crimson paint into one palette and some yellow paint into another.

Step 11. Drop two to three drops of the yellow paint into the centre of some of the flowers.

Step 12. Without washing the brush, dip it into the palette containing the crimson paint. Paint the petals of each flower, starting from the edge of each petal and working towards the centre.

spread to the edges and that there are no unpainted gaps.

Step 14. Once all areas have been covered leave the vase in the horizontal position to dry overnight.

Step 15. Trace the stamens and veins of the leaves, and touch up any areas of the outliner which might have paint on them.

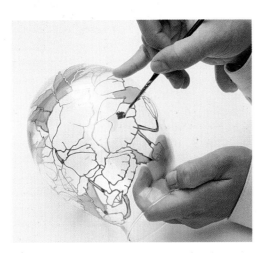

TIP:

Take care that steps 11 and 12 are done within a few minutes, because if the yellow paint dries before the red touches it, the colours will not mingle.

Step 13. Lift the object now and then to check that the colour is even and has

TIP:

If you accidentally paint over the outliner, touch the painted area with the outliner, covering the error.

Your vase is now ready.

See CARE OF PAINTED GLASSWARE earlier in this chapter.

Choose a vase with a relatively simple shape, and one inside which the design can be easily secured. If the vase has too many curves and grooves, it may be difficult to secure the design and you might have to choose a design which can be divided into smaller pieces to secure it properly. I personally prefer keeping the design inside the vase as a guide to the pattern.

PROJECT 8: FLOATING CANDLE HOLDER

CREATING A SEA HORSE DESIGN

Decorating a floating candle holder using masking tape and sponging.

Random textural effects can be achieved by applying paint with a textured object rather than a more conventional implement like a brush or knife. A sponge or a wad of cloth is the obvious choice as these hold colour well and have pleasant surface textures.

Sponging is probably the quickest, easiest and most versatile of the various paint finishes. Ideally, the sponge should not be overloaded with paint, otherwise the marks will be too heavy. Dab repeatedly with the sponge or rag in a random fashion, turning the hand between each dab to help prevent repetition of identical marks.

A natural sponge gives the most unusual effect, although a synthetic sponger offers a greater variety of surface textures and may be cut into a shape as well. The size of the sponge should be large enough to sit comfortably in your hand.

Masking an area is the opposite of stencilling, in that the design is deliberately shielded as paint is applied, so that when this masking is removed an area of unpainted surface remains. Any material that will stick securely to the glass and not react with the paint can be used as a resist. Sticky-backed plastic, peelable stickers, masking tape and wood glue are some of the materials that can be used to mask the area.

In this project, I have combined the technique of sponging and masking to achieve this effective floating candle holder. When the candles are lit, light passes through the sponged surface as well as the transparent paint and the effects are quite stunning.

You will find that after you have used about three-quarters of an outliner tube, it tends to become difficult to use as the paste just spurts out, leaving unsightly blobs on the painted surface. I hate throwing away the tubes before they are finished, so I keep these near-empty tubes to use for sponging and other effects which do not require the paste to be squeezed through the nozzle.

MATERIALS

- One clear glass fish bowl

- Transparent glass paints (violet, red, blue and green)

- 1 gold outliner tube

- 1 used gold outliner tube

- No. 2 synthetic or fine hair water-colour brush

- A small block of synthetic or natural sponge

- Half a square foot of self-adhesive vinyl

ACCESSORIES

- Template of design

- Scissors

- Masking tape

- Cotton buds

- Paper towel

- Craft knife

See PREPARATION and GETTING STARTED earlier in this chapter.

STEP-BY-STEP INSTRUCTIONS

Step 1. Trace the design onto the vinyl, and then cut the design.

Step 2. Stick the design randomly on the surface of the bowl.

Step 3. Cut the used outliner tube and squeeze it into the palette. Add a few drops of water and mix thoroughly with the brush until you get a smooth paste which is neither too thick nor too runny.

Step 4. Dab the sponge lightly in the paste, wipe the excess paste onto the palette and lightly sponge the bowl. Leave to dry overnight.

Step 5. Peel off the self-adhesive vinyl. The area that has been masked with the vinyl is left clear.

Step 6. Lay the bowl horizontally on the work surface and start work from the top to avoid smudges.

Step 7. Trace the design of the sea horses with the gold outliner tube, and leave to dry for a few hours.

Step 8. Pour a few drops of each the colours into individual sections of the palette.

Step 9. Paint each sea horse in the colour of your choice, taking care to clean the brush when you change the colours.

TIP:

When you have traced the outline on one side of the bowl, let the paste dry for at least 15 to 20 minutes before proceeding with the other side, so as to avoid accidental smudges.

TIP:

When you have painted the sea horses on one side of the bowl, let the paint dry for at least half an hour before proceeding with the other side, so as to avoid marking the wet paint.

Step 10. Add final touches like dots and lines to the painted sea horses with the gold outliner paste.

Your floating candle holder is now ready.

Note: The sponged paint peels off if it is not handled carefully. Take care when handling the glass and do not scrub the surface.

See CARE OF PAINTED GLASSWARE earlier in this chapter.

Note: When choosing the glass for this project, ensure that you choose glass which can withstand the heat of the candles and is suitable for a floating candle holder. Coloured glass decorated by sponging also looks very effective.

PROJECT 9: FRUIT BOWL

CREATING A GRAPE VINE COLLAGE

Decorating a fruit bowl by sticking glass nuggets to it, and using gel crystal.

Spattering is an application of thick paint which stands well clear of the painting surface. It is favoured for its texture and for its art form, as well as for its strong colours. It may be scumbled into place or applied more precisely with a brush or a knife which is well loaded with thick creamy paint. Paint can also be applied directly from the tube.

Collage is an image built up from various materials which are glued into place. Collages can be made of any material. When making a collage using glass paints I prefer using materials like glass beads, stones, sequins and so on which complement glass.

This project is a combination of spattering and collage, and here I have stuck glass gems and added glitter to the paint.

MATERIALS

- Transparent glass fruit bowl
- Violet-coloured glass nuggets
- No. 2 synthetic or fine hair water-colour brush
- One pewter outliner tube
- One black outliner tube
- Contour paste
- Transparent water-based glass paint (brown and black)

- One tube of green gel crystal (with glitter)

- Clear glass adhesive

ACCESSORIES

- Template of design

- Scissors

- Masking tape

- Cotton buds

- Paper towel

- Craft knife

See PREPARATION and GETTING STARTED earlier in this chapter.

TIP:

Start your work from the top to avoid accidental smudges.

STEP-BY-STEP INSTRUCTIONS

Step 1. Lay the bowl flat on the surface to be painted.
Step 2. Trace the outline of the trellis design with the black outliner tube, following the pattern by lightly squeezing the outliner paste, until you have covered the whole trellis.
Step 3. Let the outliner dry for approximately half an hour or so.

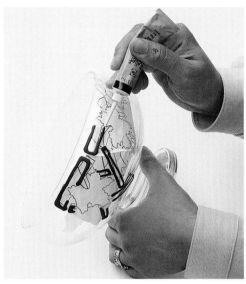

TIP:

Wipe blobs of outliner paste onto a tissue before continuing with the outline on the painting.

Step 4. Pour some contour paste into a palette and fill in the areas within the trellis with the contour paste.
Step 5. Paint the 'grape' areas with the glass adhesive, following the manufacturer's instructions.
Step 6. Secure the glass gems one at a time, sticking them to each other giving the appearance of grapes.
Step 7. Leave to dry for half a day.
Step 8. Trace the outline of the vine design with the pewter outliner paste. Apply extra pressure on the nozzle to achieve a thick outline. Trace around the grapes as well.

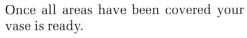

brush, drop the paint into the 'branch' areas within the design, filling them with paint. Spread the paint by using the brush to cover the area. The paint spreads easily to the outliner paste lines.

Once all areas have been covered your vase is ready.

See CARE OF PAINTED GLASSWARE earlier in this chapter.

Step 9. Leave to dry for a few hours.
Step 10. Fill in the areas within the leaf with the gel crystal directly from the nozzle.

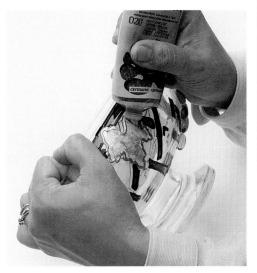

Step 11. Spread lightly with a knife to get a smooth finish.
Step 12. Pour a few drops of brown paint into the mixing palette. Using the

Note: Take care when handling the glass nuggets.

Suppliers of stained glass materials stock a variety of bevelled glass, glass nuggets and pre-cut glass pieces in various shapes and sizes which are ideal for collages. The glass nuggets can be stuck directly onto the glass by using the glass paint extender instead of an adhesive.

PROJECT 10: STORAGE JAR

CREATING A MARINE DESIGN BY MARBLING

Decorating using marbling and masking techniques, and painting on wood.

Marbling is a very easy way to decorate glass, but should be used selectively. In this project, you must use solvent-based paints. Decorating objects in this manner is great fun as it is quick to do and the effects are different every time. However, it is also messy, so protect the surrounding area very carefully before beginning the project. Marbling works best on flat surfaces.

MATERIALS

- Storage jar with flat sides

- Solvent-based transparent glass paints (turquoise, light blue, pink, light green, red, dark blue, yellow, white)

- Gold and black outliner tubes

- No. 2 synthetic or fine hair water-colour brush

- Self-adhesive vinyl

- Acrylic beads for decoration

ACCESSORIES

- Template of design

- Bowl which is larger than the storage jar

- Scissors

- Cotton buds

- Paper towel

- Craft knife

- Toothpicks

- Newspaper

PREPARATION

Protect the marbling bowl by lining it with a bin liner.

See PREPARATION and GETTING STARTED earlier in this chapter.

STEP-BY-STEP INSTRUCTIONS

Step 1. Enlarge the design and trace the design of the fish onto the self-adhesive vinyl. Cut along the outlines of the fish, and stick it randomly on the storage jar.
Step 2. Fill the marbling bowl with cold water.

Step 3. Pour a few drops of light blue paint, and a few drops of turquoise transparent paint onto the surface of the water. Stir lightly with a toothpick, separating the paint into tiny dots floating on top of the water.

Step 4. Hold the jar horizontally and dip one side of the jar into the water for a few seconds. Leave it on the nearby newspaper to drip dry.

Step 5. Repeat step 4 with the other three sides.

Step 6. Leave to dry overnight.

Step 7. Peel away the stickers, to reveal the clear area beneath.

Step 8. Trace the outline of the fish designs with the gold outliner tube.

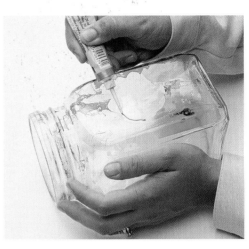

Step 9. Draw reeds randomly all over the lower half of the jar with the gold outliner tube.

Step 10. Let the outliner paste dry for a few hours.

Step 11. Paint in the reeds green.

Step 12. Pour some pink paint into the palette and some yellow paint into another palette.

Step 13. Paint the top half of the fish pink and while the paint is still wet,

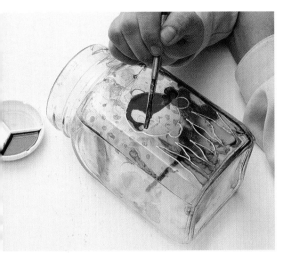

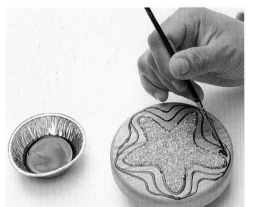

Step 4. Leaving a space of about half a centimetre (about ¼in), draw random lines around the starfish, with the black outliner tube.
Step 5. Leave to dry overnight.
Step 6. Paint the space between the lines in turquoise and light blue shades.

paint the bottom half of it yellow. The two paints will merge with each other.
Step 14. Paint some of the fish red and dark blue.
Step 15. Let the paint dry.

Decorating the Wooden Lid

Step 1. Draw a starfish in the centre of the lid with the black outliner tube.
Step 2. When the outliner is dry, fill the starfish with white glass paint, and pour the beads on top of the paint (while the paint is wet).
Step 3. Let these dry overnight.

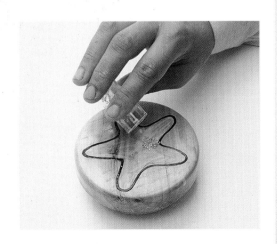

Your storage jar is now ready.

See CARE OF PAINTED GLASSWARE earlier in this chapter.

TIP:

If the wood to be painted is porous, treat it with a coat of varnish before painting on it.

PROJECT 11: RECYCLED GLASS BOTTLE

PAINTING THE ENTIRE BOTTLE

Decorating large areas with a foam brush.

There is a wide range of glassware available, but invariably we can never find the colour and shape to match our rooms. In this project you can paint entire bottles in the colour of your choice. Usually when decorating large areas with glass paints, the paint tends to streak, but if you use a thick 1in (25mm) sponge brush, you will achieve a smooth professional paint finish.

MATERIALS

- Recycled glass bottle
- Transparent glass paints (violet and light green)
- Thinner
- Extender
- Gold and silver outliner tubes
- 1in (25mm) foam brush

ACCESSORIES

- Cold soapy water
- Paper towels
- Foil cups

See PREPARATIONS and GETTING STARTED earlier in this chapter.

STEP-BY-STEP INSTRUCTIONS

Step 1. Place the bottle to be painted on the table.

Step 2. Pour approximately two capfuls of violet paint into one foil cup, add a few drops of thinner and a few drops of extender into the cup. Do not mix.

Step 3. Pour approximately one capful of light green paint into another foil cup.

Step 4. Dip the foam brush into the violet paint, and lightly paint the top half of the bottle.

Step 5. Wipe the excess paint onto a kitchen towel, dip the same brush into the green paint, and paint the remaining part of the bottle.

TIP:

The paint must be applied very lightly. This prevents the paint from dripping and streaks appearing. You could use a thick brush or cotton wool to achieve the same result, but a consistent effect is achieved by using the foam brush.

Step 6. The two paints merge and a shaded effect is achieved.

Step 7. Leave the bottle to dry overnight, before decorating with gold outliner.

WATCH POINT

As you can see, the quantity of paint required here is far more than for any other project. The best way to economize on this sort of project is to gather together all the bottles that need painting in a similar colour, and then paint them in one session. This not only saves on paint, but also on tidying up later.

See CARE OF PAINTED GLASSWARE earlier in this chapter.

Note: Do not soak the painted glassware in water. The paint chips easily, so you might want to coat it with a thin layer of varnish. Use only the manufacturer's recommended varnish. Refer to VARNISHING earlier in this chapter before proceeding with varnishing the bottles.

The bottles can be decorated with abstract or geometrical designs made with the outliner tube. Add glitter, gems and so on to decorate the bottles. A trellis design looks very attractive. Take care when decorating with the outliner, because if you need to correct any errors the paint might peel off in the process.

PROJECT 12: PAINTING VAN GOGH'S 'IRISES'

Imitating the paintings of famous artists and painting large areas.

When I started glass painting, little did I realize that one day I would be painting a 'Van Gogh'! Like most people, I have always been frightened of painting on a blank canvas, for fear of making a mess of things. The advantage of painting on glass is that any errors can be rectified without wastage of the supports. As can be seen from the earlier projects, all minor errors can be rectified immediately, by cleaning with a cotton bud or scraping with a craft knife when dry. You can also clean minor errors with a cotton bud soaked in the thinner. However, if you are completely dissatisfied with the painting, then soak the glass in warm soapy water. The paint will peel away in a couple of hours, and any residue can be scraped away.

The other great advantage of glass painting is that once you have chosen the picture of your choice, all you have to do is enlarge or reduce the picture, place it underneath your glass and start painting.

MATERIALS

- ◆ 10 × 12in (25 × 30cm) glass sheet in a suitable frame

- ◆ Transparent solvent-based glass paints (light green, dark green, yellow, golden yellow, brown, light blue, dark blue, black and white)

- ◆ Thinner

- ◆ Black outliner tube

- No. 2 fine hair watercolour brush
- No. 7 thick brush

ACCESSORIES

- Template of design
- Two sheets of tracing paper, cut to fit the frame
- Sheets of white paper, cut to fit the frame

- Cold soapy water
- Scissors
- Masking tape
- Cotton buds
- Paper towel
- Craft knife
- Foil cups

See PREPARATION and GETTING STARTED earlier in this chapter.

TIP:

It is easier to paint if you enlarge or reduce the painting in colour, although if you are confident you could use a black and white copy.

STEP-BY-STEP INSTRUCTIONS

Step 1. Choose the design and then enlarge or reduce it according to the size of the frame.

Step 2. Secure the design on the sheet of white paper with masking tape. Place the glass sheet on top of the design and secure it with masking tape.

Step 3. Trace the outline of the design with the black outliner tube, following the pattern by lightly squeezing the outliner paste, until you have covered the whole design.

Step 4. Let it dry overnight.

Step 5. Pour capfuls of light green, dark green and yellow paints into individual foil cups.

Step 6. With a thin brush, paint the leaves in the picture, mixing the colours as you go along. When changing colours, wipe the brush, but do not clean it in the brush cleaner. Allow the paints to mingle randomly with each other.

Step 7. After you have completed painting all the leaves of the irises, clean the brush thoroughly in the brush cleaner.

Step 8. Pour capfuls of dark blue, light blue, yellow, golden yellow and white paint into individual foil cups.

Step 9. Paint the white areas first.

Step 10. Add yellow to the white where necessary, then paint the centres of the irises yellow (as in the picture).

Step 11. Now paint in the irises with the blue shades. Add white to the blue where necessary.

Step 12. Leave the painting to dry for a few hours.

Step 13. Pour a few drops of brown and white paint into individual foil cups.

Step 14. With a thick brush dab the paints randomly onto the glass, covering only the areas that should be brown.

TIP:

Use the picture for guidance.

Step 15. Leave the painting to dry overnight.

Step 16. Place the glass into the frame and place this over the picture for guidance.

TIP:

The advantage of doing this is that when the glass is turned in order to paint the background, the glass doesn't touch the paper, and it remains secure in the frame. If the paint touches the paper, the paper tends to stick to the out-liner, so by placing the glass in the frame, this problem is overcome.

TIP:

The best way to achieve the 'look' is by first dabbing on the white paint for the white flowers in the background, then the golden yellow, then the yellow and then the green.

TIP:

Ideally, you should complete the background within an hour or so. Once you have started painting, continue until you have finished the background, as the picture tends to look uneven if the paint dries before the background is complete.

Step 17. Pour capfuls of green, yellow, golden yellow and white paint into individual foil cups.

Step 18. With a thick brush, cover the background with these colours, keeping the picture as a guide. Only cover the areas that are in the background and do not worry if the paints merge with each other. Wipe rather than clean the brushes between change of colours.

Step 19. Once you have completed the background, leave it to dry for at least 24 hours.

Step 20. Place the two sheets of tracing paper over the glass, between the back of the painting and the board of the frame, and then fix the backing of the frame into place.

Your painting is now ready.

CARE INSTRUCTIONS

An easy way to protect a painting on glass is to sandwich it between a sheet of glass and the frame backing, thereby never exposing the painting to the elements.

Working on flat surfaces is easier than working on vertical surfaces. You can either imitate the work of artists like Klimt, Picasso, and so on, or create your very own work of art.

PROJECT 13: ISLAMIC PAINTING

A painting inspired by Islamic art and introducing the use of gold leaf.

In this project I have combined the use of geometric patterns, calligraphy and gold leaf. The colours usually associated with glass painting are bright and vibrant, but in this project I have used the extender to achieve pale shades.

MATERIALS

- Transparent solvent-based glass paints (green, brown, white and violet)

- Extender

- Thinner

- Black, gold and silver outliner tubes

- One easy metal (i.e. gold leaf) sheet

- Thick soft brush suitable to tamp down the leaf metal

- One bottle of varnish

- One bottle of adhesive

- No. 2 fine hair watercolour brush

- No. 2 fine hair brush (old brush)

- Suitable frame with two sheets of glass to fit frame

- Art paper cut to the size of the frame

STEP-BY-STEP INSTRUCTIONS

Step 1. Enlarge the design to the size of the frame.

Step 2. Secure the design on the sheet of white paper with masking tape. Place the glass sheet on top of the design and secure it with masking tape.

Step 3. Apply the adhesive as you would apply paint, taking care that it does not spill or drip, covering the area of the calligraphy only.

Step 4. Leave the adhesive to dry for at least 15 minutes.

Step 5. Gently lay on the gold leaf and tamp down with a soft brush. Allow to dry for at least 2 to 3 hours.

Step 6. Using a thick, soft hair paintbrush, brush in the leaf metal, making circular movements; collect the excess leaf in an old newspaper or container.

TIP:

The gold leaf will adhere to areas where adhesive has been applied. Therefore take great care that the adhesive is applied only to areas where you want the gold leaf, and clean anywhere that the adhesive has accidentally spread to.

ACCESSORIES

- Template of design

- Masking tape

- Cotton buds

- Paper towel

- Craft knife

See PREPARATIONS and GETTING STARTED earlier in this chapter.

Step 7. Clean the glass with great care, ensuring that all excess particles of the gold leaf have been removed from the glass.

Step 8. Trace the outline of the calligraphy with the black outliner.

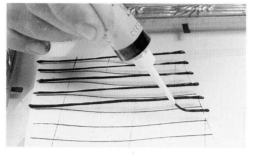

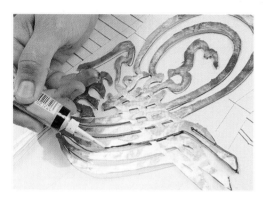

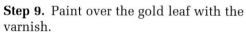

Step 9. Paint over the gold leaf with the varnish.

Step 10. Make pale olive green paint in a palette by mixing green, brown and the extender in approximately the following proportions: ten drops of extender, three drops of green and one drop of brown.

Step 11. Using the brush, drop a few drops of paint at a time on the area to be painted. It will spread easily with a little help from the brush.

Step 12. Let the picture dry for at least two hours

Step 13. Pour the extender into a palette. Add a few drops of violet, to get a pale lilac colour. Follow step 11 until you have covered all the areas that have to be painted violet. Let the paint dry for a few hours.

Step 14. With the black outliner, trace the trellis area of the design. Leave to dry for a few hours.

Step 15. Fill in alternate squares with brown paint and then when dry fill in the remaining squares with white paint.

Step 16. Trace the outline of the design with gold outliner, and when dry add a second layer with the silver outliner. Let the outliner dry.

Step 17. Place the unpainted sheet of glass inside the frame, then place the painted sheet of glass over it, taking care that the painted surface faces the right side of the frame.

Step 18. Place a sheet of suitable art paper to give a background to the frame, before placing the backing of the frame. Your painting is now ready.

CARE INSTRUCTIONS

Since the painting is sandwiched between a sheet of glass and the frame backing, it is well protected and cannot be easily damaged.

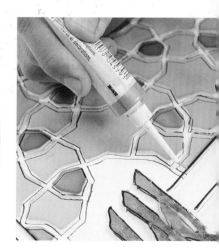

PROJECT 14: LAMPSHADE

VICTORIA AND ALBERT MUSEUM-INSPIRED PROJECT

Making a simple but effective lampshade, inspired by traditional stained glass designs.

The lamp in this project was inspired by twelfth- or early thirteenth-century stained glass from Canterbury Cathedral which is displayed at the Victoria and Albert Museum in London. The V & A Museum is known internationally as a great museum of the decorative arts. It has a wide range of items in all areas of design from around the world. These provide a source of inspiration for all artists.

The lamp is very simple to make and all you need is a piece of glass cut to the size of your choice. If you cannot cut the glass yourself, then the best way to overcome this problem is to draw the cartoon and ask your local glazier to cut and polish the glass to fit. In this project I have used textured glass.

MATERIALS

- 2mm-thick textured glass cut to shape as per template

- Lamp base with light bulb and fittings

- Transparent glass paints (red, blue, green, yellow), solvent or water-based

- Black outliner tube

- Contour paste

- No. 2 synthetic or fine hair watercolour brush

- No. 1 thin brush

ACCESSORIES

- Template of design

- Template of the shape to which the glass has to be cut

- Masking tape

- Cotton buds

- Paper towel

- Craft knife

- Cold soapy water

See PREPARATIONS and GETTING STARTED earlier in this chapter.

STEP-BY-STEP INSTRUCTIONS

Step1. Place the design in position, under the surface to be painted, using masking tape to hold it in place.

Step 2. Lay the glass piece on top of the design and secure it in place with masking tape.

Step 3. Trace the outline of the design with the outliner tube, following the pattern by lightly squeezing the outliner paste, until you have covered the whole design, as well as the brush marks within the design.

Step 4. Let the outliner paste dry for approximately half an hour or so.

Step 5. Paint in the red coloured areas, filling them with paint. Using the brush, the paint will spread easily to the outliner paste lines. The outliner paste will hold the colour separately, giving the appearance of individual pieces of glass.

TIP:

The outline should be thick.

TIP:

If the paint accidentally spills or spreads, wipe it immediately with a soft moist cloth or tissue and it will come clean.

Step 6. The paint takes approximately 10 to 15 minutes to partially dry but about a day to harden.

Step 7. Wash the brush thoroughly, and then pour some blue paint into the palette and fill in the blue areas with the paint.

Step 8. Lift the object now and then to check that the colour is even and has spread to the edges and that there are no unpainted gaps.

Step 9. Continue in a similar fashion, colouring in the green and yellow areas.

Step 10. Leave the glass to dry overnight.

TIP:

If you accidentally paint over the outliner, touch the painted area with the outliner, covering the error.

Step 11. With the contour paste and a thin brush, lightly paint in the thin black lines, so as to give the appearance of traditional painted glass.

Step 12. Leave to dry overnight.

Step 13. Fix into the lamp holder.

Your lampshade is now ready.

The painted shade looks extremely attractive when the light shines through it.

See CARE OF PAINTED GLASSWARE earlier in this chapter.

PROJECT 15: FROSTING SUGAR BOWLS

CREATING WEDDING BELLS, HEARTS AND STARS USING FROSTING PAINT

Decorating sugar bowls using water-based frosting paints and adding glitter to decorate.

Traditionally, frosting is achieved by using hydrofluoric acid, which basically eats away at the glass to give a frosted look. However, with the advent of water-based 'frosting' paints, you can recreate the effect of frosted surfaces. The frosting paints work in the same way as the transparent glass paints. There is a wide variety of frosting paints available, including sprays and creams.

The sugar bowls in this project have been decorated using frosting cream and glitter has been added to the bowls to provide the extra sparkle.

MATERIALS

- ◆ Assorted transparent sugar bowls

- ◆ Paint Magic frosting medium

- ◆ Silver outliner tube

- ◆ Polyester glitter

- ◆ No. 2 synthetic watercolour brush

ACCESSORIES

- ◆ Template of design

- ◆ Scissors

- ◆ Masking tape

- ◆ Cotton buds

- ◆ Paper towel

◆ Craft knife

◆ Cold soapy w

See PREPARATION and GETTING STARTED earlier in this chapter.

STEP-BY-STEP INSTRUCTIONS

Step 1. Place the design on the inside of the bowl and secure it in place with masking tape.

Step 2. Trace the outline of the design with silver outliner paste. Sprinkle some polyester glitter on the outliner paste. Let it settle for a few minutes, then blow the excess away, taking care that you do not touch the outliner paste. Let it dry overnight.

TIP:

If the frosting medium or outliner accidentally spills or spreads, wipe it immediately with a soft moist cloth or tissue.

Step 3. Pour some frosting medium into a palette, add a drop of water, and stir it thoroughly. With the brush, fill in the areas within the design with the frosting medium as you would do with glass paints. Let it dry overnight.

Your sparkling sugar bowls are ready.

Note: The frosting medium is suitable for decorative purposes only, so take care that food does not touch the painted areas.

TIP:

The glitter tends to stick to any moist surface, therefore it is advisable to do this step out of doors.

See CARE OF PAINTED GLASSWARE earlier in this chapter.

You can cover glasses, vases, windows and any other type of glass in a similar fashion. A wide range of designs from simple motifs to elaborate patterns can be achieved by anyone, including a totally frosted glass effect on windows. However, if you are covering large areas with the frosting paint then use a foam brush to cover the area.

PROJECT 16: FROSTING ON MIRRORS

BALLET SHOES AND TRAINERS DESIGN

Decorating mirrors using stencils and a frosting spray.

Mirrors for many centuries have served both a functional and a decorative purpose, being employed at the dressing table for personal use and displayed in interiors to reflect light and give the illusion of space. A mirror is far more than just a mere looking glass – it is one of the most beautiful objects developed by man. In this project, a ready-shaped mirror is decorated using a frosting spray and stencils.

MATERIALS

◆ Two mirrors

◆ Glass etch spray

ACCESSORIES

◆ Template of design

◆ Self-adhesive vinyl

◆ Scissors

◆ Cold soapy water

◆ Paper towel

◆ Craft knife

See PREPARATIONS and GETTING STARTED earlier in this chapter.

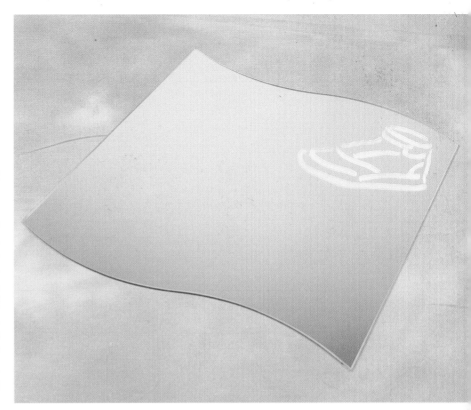

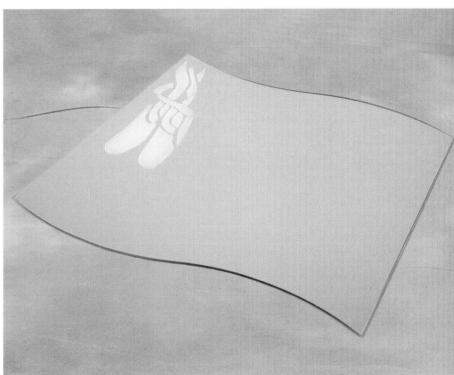

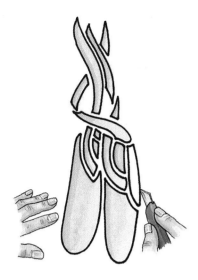

STEP-BY-STEP INSTRUCTIONS

Step 1. Enlarge the template to the appropriate size, and trace the design onto the self-adhesive vinyl. Cut the stencil with the craft knife.

TIP:

You can use ready-cut stencils, but take care that they are fixed properly to the surface before using the frosting spray.

Step 2. Stick the stencil in position on the mirror.
Step 3. Spray the glass etch directly from the can onto the cut-out areas of the stencil.
Step 4. Leave to dry for a few hours.
Step 5. Peel off the adhesive vinyl.

TIP:

Take care that the spray does not spill onto other areas of the glass. If it does, clean it immediately with a moist kitchen towel.

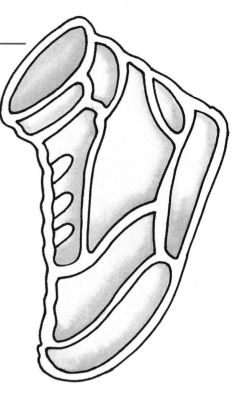

Your frosted mirror is ready.

See CARE OF PAINTED GLASSWARE earlier in this chapter.

You can decorate windows, doors and any other flat surfaces in a similar manner. But the frosting medium, unlike hydrofluoric acid, is not permanent and hence if exposed to the elements for a long period of time will peel away.

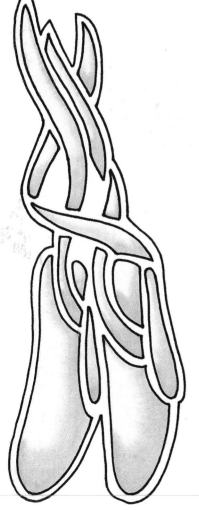

PROJECT 17: STAINED GLASS WINDOW

BIRD CAGE DESIGN

Decorating a window with self-adhesive lead and glass paints.

Many houses have odd angles or neglected corners which can be given new character with stained glass. An imaginative and daring eye will find such spots, and a room can be elevated from the ordinary into a warm, multidimensional space through the clever use of painted glass. The design need not be elaborate or complicated. A simple design with an attractive colour combination is ideal for painted glass windows. In this project I have painted a window imitating the art of stained glass.

Even though the quality of glass paints available today is very good and they do not fade easily, I would still prefer not to use the paints directly on glass which is exposed to the elements, because with time the paints will fade and peel. But if the painted surface is sandwiched between the two pieces of glass as shown in this project, then you will have none of the problems associated with exposure to the elements. Besides, the other advantage is that you can achieve the most intricate patterns when decorating windows with glass paints. You would have to be a very highly skilled glass artist if you wanted to achieve a similar effect in stained glass.

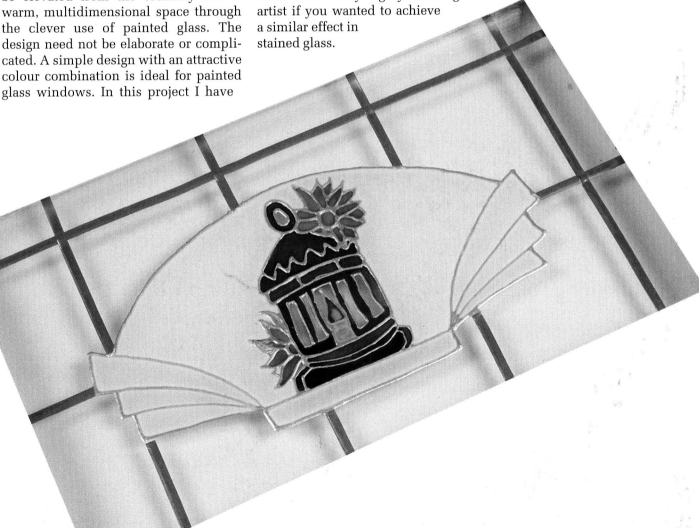

MATERIALS

- Solvent-based transparent glass paints (crimson, violet, white, green, yellow, orange)

- Thinner

- Extender

- No. 2 fine hair watercolour brush

- Pewter outliner tube

- Self-adhesive lead

- 4mm glass cut to the size of the window

- Glass adhesive

- Half inch nails

- Putty

ACCESSORIES

- Template of design

- Scissors

- Masking tape

- Cotton buds

- Paper towel

- Craft knife

- Boning peg

- Palette

PREPARATIONS

Step 1. Measure the inside of the window where you would like to place the stained glass design.

Step 2. Ask a glazier to cut the glass and polish the edges to the required size. I prefer using a 4mm thick window glass, but you could use a thicker or a thinner glass as you prefer.

Step 3. Enlarge or reduce the design to the appropriate size.

See GETTING STARTED earlier in this chapter.

STEP-BY-STEP INSTRUCTIONS

Step 1. Place the design on the work surface and secure it with masking tape. Place the glass on top of the design, and use masking tape to secure it.

Step 2. Trace the outline of the design with the outliner tube, following the pattern by lightly squeezing the outliner paste, until you have covered the whole design.

Step 3. Let the outliner dry overnight.

Step 4. Remove a sufficient length of the self-adhesive lead and carefully smooth between finger and thumb before detaching the backing paper. Stretch the lead slightly.

Step 5. Carefully remove the backing paper. Place one end at the starting point and press firmly onto the glass. Guide the lead into place along the trellis line, applying finger pressure to the end where the lead is cut.

Step 6. Secure the self-adhesive lead onto the glass using the boning peg, applying a firm, even pressure. First run the flat edge of the peg along the full length of the top surface and then using the concave-formed end of the peg, traverse the full length of the strip. Finally, using the pointed end, holding the peg at an approximate angle of 45 degrees, run the peg along both the outer edges of the strip in a firm, smooth action, crimping the lead to the glass. Repeat on each strand and treat all joints in the same manner, ensuring that no gaps are left between the lead and the glass. Correct boning ensures permanent adhesion.

Step 7. Pour a few drops of white paint into the mixing palette. Add a drop of yellow and mix well. Using the brush,

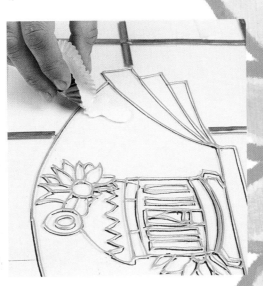

drop the paint into the 'candle' area within the design, filling it with paint. Spread the paint by using the brush to cover the area.

Step 8. The paint will spread easily and the outliner paste will hold the colour separately, giving the appearance of individual pieces of glass. The paint takes approximately half an hour to dry partially but about a day to harden.

Step 9. Clean the brush thoroughly in the thinner and then pour some extender into the palette. Add a few drops of violet to the extender. Vary the colour according to your choice, and fill in the 'cage' areas with the paint.

Step 10. Lift the glass now and then to check that the colour is even and has spread to the edges and that there are no unpainted gaps.

Step 11. Colour the centre of the flame in orange, and add yellow to the rest of the flame. Continue in a similar fashion, filling in all the areas that have to be painted. All the colours mix well and you can get different shades by mixing the paints.

Step 12. Let the painted glass dry for a couple of days. Ensure that it is in a dust-free environment.

COMPLETING THE PROJECT

Step 1. Ensure that both the window where the glass is to be fixed as well as the painted glass are clean and free of any fingerprints or dust particles.

Step 2. Using the glass adhesive, stick the painted glass onto the window. The painted surface should be sandwiched between the two sheets of glass.

Step 3. Hammer the nails into the window frame to secure the glass.

Step 4. Putty the window, following the manufacturer's instructions on puttying.

PROJECT 18: DOUBLE-GLAZED WINDOW

GEOMETRIC DESIGN

Decorating a double-glazed window with glass paints.

Traditionally, windows are the great 'canvas' of glass art. As the primary source of light, windows are intrinsically the focal point of a room and the urge to play with that light is irresistible. The thin, airy surface of the glass, breaking the mass of the impenetrable wall, invites design and decoration. Strong, bright colours and complex designs can overpower a room, but simple stained glass designs can be extremely effective. When choosing a design for a window, you must consider not only the effect of light falling through the coloured glass, but also decorative beauty, so that a passer-by, not seeing the light effects, would find pleasure in the colour and composition of the window.

Double-glazed windows are becoming more and more common now and combining the modern window with stained glass is taking on a whole new dimension.

In this project, I have painted the inside of the window which is sealed between the two layers of glass.

You would need the assistance of a double-glazing window specialist to complete this project.

MATERIALS

- Glass piece cut to the size of the window frame

- Solvent-based transparent glass paints

- Black outliner tube

- No. 2 fine hair watercolour brush

ACCESSORIES

- Template of design

- Scissors

- Masking tape

- Cotton buds

- Paper towel

- Craft knife

- Glass cleaning liquid

See PREPARATION *earlier in this chapter.*

GETTING STARTED

Step 1. Protect your clothes with an apron or an old shirt, and cover your work surface with an old cloth or papers. Your work surface should be positioned at a comfortable height, and should be clear of everything other than the items you are going to need when painting.

Step 2. The surface that you are painting on must be free of dust particles and grease.

Step 3. Peel off any labels and wipe all traces of adhesive.

Step 4. Clean the glass thoroughly with the glass cleaning fluid, wipe all watermarks before you start painting on it, and clean off any fingermarks with the kitchen towel.

STEP-BY-STEP INSTRUCTIONS

Step 1. Place the design in position on the work top and secure it with masking tape.

Step 2. Lay the glass sheet in position above the design, and secure the sheet with masking tape, so that it does not move.

TIP:

Ideally, you should work on a glass-top table which is lit from underneath, so that you can see the effect of light while painting. A table similar to the ones used by stained glass artists is ideal for the purpose.

Step 3. Trace the outline of the design with the black outliner tube, following the pattern by lightly squeezing the outliner paste, until you have covered the whole design.

Step 4. Let the outliner dry for approximately half an hour or so.

TIP:

The design should be positioned at least 1in (25mm) away from the edges of the glass. This is essential for double-glazing.

TIP:

Wipe blobs of outliner paste onto a tissue before continuing with the outline on the window, as this will help to give a neat finish.

Step 5. Colour in the design with colours of your choice.

Step 6. Take care to see that the colour has spread to the edges and that there are

TIP:

If there is an accident with the outliner, clean it immediately with a moist cloth or let it dry overnight and then scrape it off carefully with a craft knife.

no unpainted gaps between the paint and the outliner paste. If possible lift the glass now and then to check that the colour is even and has spread to the edges and that there are no unpainted gaps.

TIP:

If the paint accidentally spills or spreads, wipe it immediately with a soft moist cloth or tissue.

Step 7. Once the whole design has been painted in, leave to dry overnight.

Step 8. Clean the glass thoroughly before sending it to be double-glazed.

WATCH POINT

◆ The painted surface should be sandwiched between the glass.

◆ The window can now be fitted in position.

TIP:

If you accidentally paint over the outliner, touch the painted area with the outliner, covering the error.

Useful Addresses

Glass Art Ltd
75 Coniston Gardens
Kingsbury
London
NW9 0BA
UK
(suppliers of all your glass painting
needs by mail order)

Lead and Light
35a Hartland Road
London
NW1 4DB
UK
(Stained glass suppliers)

Victoria and Albert Museum
160 Brompton Road
London
SW3 1HW
UK
(Museum)

MANUFACTURERS

Decra Led
Newton Moor Industrial Estate
Mill Street
Hyde
Cheshire
SK14 4LJ
UK

Deka Textilfarben GmbH
Kappellenstraße 18
D 82008
Unterhaching
Germany

Pebeo
Avenue du Pic de Bertagne
BP106 – 13881
Gemenos cedex
France

Staedtler (UK) Ltd
Pontyclun
Mid Glamorgan
CF72 8YJ
UK

Index